"Rachel's joy in sharing her own experience for others' benefit never ceases to amaze me. She is a selfless sharer with wisdom that cannot be ignored. Her message is eloquently outlined in *Relentless Joy* and reaches all readers to their core. It's rare that a book actually makes you a better human, but that's exactly what this one does. Soak up this guidance willingly to put into action throughout your life."

Laura Rutledge, ESPN host and reporter

"*Relentless Joy* is a fantastic glance into Rachel Baribeau's journey. Just like her annual talks with our football team, you can feel Rachel's positive perspective, genuine passion, and abundant joy, even in the face of adversity, as you read her book. This book is another elite benchmark in Rachel's mission of #ImChangingtheNarrative."

P.J. Fleck, University of Minnesota head football coach

"The first time I heard Rachel speak I immediately wished that I had known her when I was coaching. I would certainly have had her come speak to our players and promoted her speaking to our entire student body. Her message is truly that prominent.

I've always encouraged the young men in our football program to 'surround themselves with people who can and will make their lives better.' At the top of that list, for me, is Rachel Baribeau. She makes a difference in a most positive way. Her words, as you will read, will strongly and positively impact your life. She has a passion for bringing a productive, joyful, meaningful, and helpful life to others.

Relentless Joy is a fantastic read for all ages. And all who read or hear Rachel speak regarding 'changing the narrative' will benefit tremendously and have access to a more productive and fruitful life. It is also a guide to the development of prominent, caring, and successful leadership. I find myself drawing daily from her thoughts written in this book, feeling as though it has made my life better."

Bill Snyder, College Football Hall of Fame coach

"*Relentless Joy* is an open reservoir of passion. Rachel is a true ambassador of the ferocious authenti̇̇̇ the heart of any audience. Rachel and now she has arrived to deliver yourself a favor and jump on the j̇̇̇

David Tyree, Super Bowl cḣ̇̇

RELENTLESS
JOY

RELENTLESS
JOY

Finding Freedom, Passion, and Happiness
(Even When You Have to Fight for It)

RACHEL JOY BARIBEAU

Revell
a division of Baker Publishing Group
Grand Rapids, Michigan

Published by Revell
a division of Baker Publishing Group
Grand Rapids, Michigan
www.revellbooks.com

Printed in the United States of America

Library of Congress Cataloging-in-Publication Data
Names: Baribeau, Rachel Joy, author.
Title: Relentless joy : finding freedom, passion, and happiness (even when you have to fight for it) / Rachel Joy Baribeau.
Description: Grand Rapids, Michigan : Revell, a division of Baker Publishing Group, [2023] | Includes bibliographical references.
Identifiers: LCCN 2022043989 | ISBN 9780800742478 (paperback) | ISBN 9780800743062 (casebound) | ISBN 9781493441228 (ebook)
Subjects: LCSH: Joy.
Classification: LCC BF575.H27 B365 2023 | DDC 158—c23/eng/20230120
LC record available at https://lccn.loc.gov/2022043989

Published in association with The Bindery Agency, www.TheBinderyAgency.com.

Baker Publishing Group publications use paper produced from sustainable forestry practices and post-consumer waste whenever possible.

23   24   25   26   27   28   29   7   6   5   4   3   2   1

To my Booty-Tooty and number one fan, my mommy. I did it, we did it! Can you believe it? I know you are throwing a party in heaven for this book. Can you and Jesus let some confetti fall down here on us?

And to my soulmate and best friend, Christopher William Rohe. Thank you for your endless support! None of this would be possible without you. You are my best friend and the answer to my prayers. I've been called a lot of beautiful names in my life, but "wife" means the most to me. I love you over the Grand Tetons and back.

To my (bonus) kids. Thank you for making my life more amazing than I could ever fathom.

And to my people: my family, my friends, and my fans that have become friends. You complete me, and I mean it, every bit as cheesy as it sounds. If you have ever wished me well or prayed for me, count yourself amongst my tribe.

Parts of this book are hard to read. There is mention of self-harm, suicide, and other sensitive topics. I want to be respectful and thoughtful to everyone that will dive into these pages by including an overall trigger warning. But hear me when I say this—feel it deeply, and maybe even close your eyes and say it to yourself—even in the midst of my triggers, there is joy waiting to be discovered. I love you.

Contents

Introduction 11

1. The Birth of a Movement 19
2. People First 31
3. On a Hill in Africa 41
4. Don't Look Away 51
5. The Gift of Pain 63
6. The Garden Tomb 75
7. The Prodigal Daughter 89
8. The Power of Vulnerability 99
9. Feed Your Soul 111
10. The Pity Kiddie Pool 121
11. My Father's Table 133
12. In His Time 143
13. Miracles in Disguise 157
14. It Starts with a YES! 167
15. Your Ancestors 179
16. No Coincidences 189

Conclusion 201
Acknowledgments 205
Notes 209
Journaling Space 213

Introduction

What follows are my innermost thoughts. I have spent the better part of a year putting them on paper, but they have been percolating my entire life. And before you dive in, let me just say that as excited as I am for you to read this and hopefully be changed, I am also completely terrified. I make a living from being vulnerable, but, holy cow, this is a new level, even for me. But if I didn't offer you my full self in these pages, I'd be missing the point of this book entirely.

So this is Rachel: completely raw and unabridged.

In this book, I humbly offer you my story. Not just for the sake of telling it but to share what I have been blessed with in hopes that you will discover it too.

And what's that, you might ask?

Joy.

Through the many ups and downs of my journey, I have discovered a joy that is like that sturdy old umbrella standing strong against the wind. The kind of joy that is battle-tested and maybe a little beat-up, but you know it's going to hold in the worst tempest. Yep, my friend, that is what you stand to procure from this book. An unwavering and relentless joy.

Maybe you feel like I once did: hopeless or in a perpetual funk. Maybe you've hit rock bottom financially, spiritually, or psychologically. Maybe you just know there is more. I've been there. I've been all these places and I'm telling you, you are exactly where you are meant to be, holding or listening to this book. There is a plan to move forward, and I believe with all my heart that the baby steps to help get you there are within these pages.

But before I get too far ahead, let me tell you a little about myself. I was adopted by my father at eighteen months old, told at six, and then retold at twelve, since I didn't remember. This revelation pulled the rug out from under my little soul's feet. I hid the sadness, telling no one. I was internally calling myself names like *bastard*, *unwanted*, and *unloved*. (Well, I think Satan was the author of those lies, but we will save that for a bit later.)

At twenty, I was pistol-whipped and almost raped in an attempted robbery/murder. I fought back and put all four perpetrators in jail, two for twenty years apiece. (They had very long, violent rap sheets.) I battled an addiction to hard drugs through most of my twenties, which eventually led to selling the drug to support my habit. Even as I was ascending in the sportscasting world, I was battling this addiction—literally living a double life. I got clean in 2008 only by the grace of God and have never looked back.

I was the first and only known female sportscaster to ever fully participate in a semi- or professional football training camp. I lasted for five days of two-a-days before being medically released. (The plan was never to play in a game, only to learn it from the inside out. I was beaten black and blue after seven days of being tackled. I was a walking ice pack.)

I've climbed the world's tallest freestanding mountain, Kilimanjaro. I organized the group climb on behalf of my dear friend and former NFL player Kevin Turner in support of his battle with ALS. We encountered a blizzard at the top. I slipped and fell while on the Western Breach and started to slide very quickly. The last person in line on the climb grabbed me midfall. I count myself as a miracle, having survived that slip on the top of that mountain. (Sidenote: the person who caught me was added to the climb the night before. Coincidence? I don't believe in them. But more on that later.)

I was the first female host on SiriusXM collegiate sports stations, was on the jumbotron of the Cowboys stadium highlighting college football history and hosting the first College Football Playoff game, and am one of the few females in the world to vote on the prestigious Heisman award, which is awarded to the best player in college football. (Let's go, girls!)

I've faced pain that I wouldn't wish on anyone. (Sadly, I'm sure many of you can relate.) I've survived abuse in my childhood and in my adult relationships. I've since done major work through therapy and with Jesus to forgive. I left that toxicity in my past, deciding that the cycle ends with me. I have lost both my parents and so many others. Grief is a constant companion, but I've made peace with it. Sort of. I almost took my own life after losing my mommy to cancer. I call it my Dark Night of the Soul, which you will hear about later in this book.

Let's all take a breath after that paragraph! Sheesh! I don't know that I've ever written all these facts about my life in one place. I am well aware that my life has been dramatic, by the way. As much as I loathe drama, it tends to follow me. Not in a dramatic "let's argue, fuss, and fight" way but in a sensational "crazy and amazing things just keep happening" way. People have often told me it should be made into a movie. (Welcome to my life.)

But please know that I share these things not for sympathy but to say that through it all, I still have joy. Joy that rumbles up from my soul, to paraphrase Maya Angelou. That's why I am so determined to spread joy. It's my calling in life. With a zillion news outlets pumping doom and gloom into our faces all day, I have made the conscious decision to be a *JOYstarter* instead. And I want to teach others to do the same.

It's with this mindset that I founded a movement called #Im ChangingtheNarrative. Our mission is to promote positive mental health and GOOD love for yourself and others by serving as inspiration for students, professionals, and parents as they create individual legacies of purpose, passion, and platform. Since its inception in 2016, we have worked with more than sixty colleges multiple times, law enforcement in several states, US Customs and Border Protection, high schools, prison ministry, churches, and halfway houses. When I am discouraged, my business manager reminds me that I created this from nothing. From an idea in my mind and a calling in my soul.

In this book, you will learn many of the same principles I teach from stages across the country. Recently, one of our leaders and speakers in #ImChangingtheNarrative, Tre Hicks, compared us to the famous explorers Lewis and Clark, charting new territory. I felt that in the deepest part of my soul. Yep! That's what we are doing, charting new territory so that others can follow, so that *you* can follow!

Hence, the writing of this book. It is an extension of my calling.

I want to teach you, my dear reader, how to have joy no matter your circumstances. I want to help you chase and notice joy in our ever-darkening world. I hope you "think, feel, and then do something about it," as my friend Tim Shaw says. If I encourage you to think and feel but you don't take action, then what is it all for? You will hear me talk about your spiritual shovel in this book. Often, we wish hard for change but are unwilling to do the digging and hard work needed to make it happen. You will need your shovel. Hard work is required for true transformation, my dear.

My mom used to tell me that a wound will get worse before it gets better. I think it's the same with transformation and healing. It is very likely to get harder and hurt worse before it gets better. But isn't the hope of healing better than sitting on the sidelines—or on the couch—always wondering what could have been?

We won't be doing things halfway in the pages of this book or in our lives. No more playing it safe or living in fear. I hope to inspire you to take action toward finding the freedom, passion, and happiness you were made for—even when you have to fight for it! As my warrior-queen and friend Thea Wood says, "Kick fear in the face!" HIYAHH!

I promise you this fight is worth it!

In this way we become the light makers in our world. The peace-keepers. The healers. The changers of the narrative.

So, are you in?

If you are still reading, I'm going to assume your answer to that question is "Heck YES!" Or maybe it's just "I'm interested. Keep talking." Either way, I am happy that you're joining me!

But before going on, there are a few things you'll need to know. First and most importantly, I love you! I want you to know that. I'm not a "love ya" person, by the way. You know, that whole "I don't know you that well, so it's only a 'ya' and not a definite 'you.'" That feels halfway to me, and as I've mentioned before, I don't do half-ways. I may not know you, but I DO love you. I love you because you are my sister, you are my brother. I love you because you are a fellow miracle and warrior. I love you because we are all on this journey together, sweet pea.

(Oh, also, I might call you *all* the pet names throughout this book because I love pet names. I gush when called sweet pea, darling heart, lovebug, sugarplum, my love. If you don't prefer them, feel free to keep hearing "dear reader" as I speak to you in the coming pages.)

Next, know that I laughed and cried a ton while writing this book. Both acts are ways to express what is going on in our hearts and are incredibly important in the healing process. Interestingly, a woman named Rose-Lynn Fisher did a multiyear photography project of more than one hundred actual tears as seen under a microscope that she captured from herself and volunteers, even a newborn. Tears elicited from grief or joy, called psychic tears, have been found to contain protein-based hormones, including the neurotransmitter leucine enkephalin, a natural painkiller that is excreted when the body is under distress. I love this quote from Rose-Lynn Fisher:

> Tears are the medium of our most primal language in moments as
> unrelenting as death, as basic as hunger and as complex as a rite of

passage. It's as though each one of our tears carries a microcosm of the collective human experience, like one drop of an ocean.[1]

So keep those tears coming! They are part of what it means to be human! I hereby give you permission to cry and laugh your heart out. Consider it a royal decree.

I also encourage you to journal and plan a book club with your neighbor, coworker, and bestie from high school. Because in truth I hope this book is received as part book, part journal. In fact, if this book were a meal, it would be a whole smorgasbord of self-help, wisdom, encouragement, and faith running together like gravy oozing out and covering all the foods on your plate. These are stories of my crazy, amazing, hard, beautiful, wonderful life. The same kind of life I want for you.

There is a JOYSTART section at the end of each chapter that offers you a practical way to apply what you are learning. It's like a jump start for your car but for your soul! Writing something down is more influential to creating lasting memories and change versus simply telling ourselves we will remember it. And sharing yourself and experiences with others creates community. There is joy, peace, understanding, support, and acceptance in community. I am no one without my people. I pray this book draws you closer to your people too.

Lastly, here is what I *know* about the journey you're about to go on: you will meet Jesus in this book. He is here among these pages, waiting to be discovered with fresh eyes. My hope is that whether you've known Him for years, been church-hurt or people-hurt, or don't believe in Him, you will get to know Him in a new way. And maybe—just maybe—after reading this book, you will want to know Him in the most intimate way! As your best friend, your provider, and your Papa. That would be the greatest joy for me! (It's also okay if you just want to learn more about Him or even if you just come to think, *Jesus seems like a pretty rad dude.*)

I mentioned my great friend Kevin who passed in 2016 from his battle with ALS. He was one of the primary inspirations for

#ImChangingtheNarrative. He once told me, "You could step off a curb tomorrow and get hit by a bus. I got a heads-up on my life. So I say I'm sorry. I hug my kids. I live life to the fullest." My gracious, what a simple yet profound mantra. Kevin loved radically and lived fully. He taught me to do the same. Now I pass this same precious knowledge on to you.

I hope when I go to be with my Maker and my mama, you will say, "That girl loved radically!" Within the pages of this book, I will teach you to love radically too. Because your life and my life are far too precious for any halfway kind of love. None of us know when our time is up, and we are all just walking each other home. I want to love radically, extraordinarily, until that moment comes. This book is an invitation to do the same in your life.

I pray you find new ways to chase joy every day and in every way, big or small. Because this moment is all we have. I once heard someone say there is a reason our windshield is so big and our rearview mirror is so small. We can't do anything about the past but learn from it, honor it, heal from it, and use it to be better. Your real gift is now. Your real gift is this book, the pencil or pen in your hand, and your desire to learn more, be more, and chase joy relentlessly!

I want you to hear and receive my words in the way that is most meaningful to you because this journey is about you! Thank you for purchasing this book, and thank you for being willing to go on the journey of a lifetime with me as your guide.

Oh, and one last gentle reminder before we set out: I love you. I see you. Your story matters greatly. I'm holding space for you!

Let's begin our journey.

CHAPTER 1

The Birth of a Movement

I am the person who runs toward trouble, to the burning building instead of away from it. And oftentimes, people are burning buildings. I know this because I was once a burning building. Heck, I still am known to spark up from time to time. But there is a difference between a life burning to the ground and a soul on fire. I want to teach you that difference. I want to teach you to look in the mirror, discern deeply, grab the fire extinguisher for yourself and others, dust the soot off your life, and ignite your soul in a whole new way.

I know it can be done. I am living proof.

Let me set the scene: it was August of 2016, and college football was breaking my heart.

I literally broke down and cried while hosting on SiriusXM College Sports Nation. I was the first female host on the college sports stations of SiriusXM, an honor that I still hold very dear. But the state of affairs of college football was so emotionally distressing to me that I penned the following article, which went viral and spawned a national movement:

Everywhere I turn these days, there is news of horrid sexual allegations, rape, blame-shifting, cheating (level 1 and 2), gross misappropriation of funds, illegal gun-toting, plausible deniability, and general lawlessness, by players and coaches.

It is not a good time for college football, and that is an understatement.

It brought up a memory I had pushed far down deep, one I had not even shared with my own family, until today. But it came barreling back like a searing-hot poker in my gut.

You see, I was once a victim (now I am a victor). Late one night I was in a familiar house with a familiar somebody, and he was uncharacteristically angry. He dragged me from one end of the house to the other, by my hair. There were other people in the house, supposedly sleeping. I screamed for help, but no one came to my aid. Finally, he relented. I curled up into a ball and went to sleep. The next day I had chunks of hair missing from my head and carpet burns covered my body. But what hurt worse than my injuries was the fact that people heard my (bloody-murder) screams, yet they refused to help me.

"Why?" When I go back to that night, that is the resounding question I have. "How could you?"

That's why I can identify with these victims at campuses across the country. I am one of them. And they are me, and a great deal of us were ignored in our most vulnerable hour.

So I will leave you with this: what are we going to do to take our game back? Where are our leaders? Our makers of men? Where are the responsible fans—you know, the ones that think for themselves rather than blindly follow their school's every decision? Where are the teammates strong enough to tell another when they are doing wrong? Where are the coaches that are willing to say, "Sometimes doing the right thing might cost me something, but I'm willing to do it!"

It's high time for these people to stand up and take the game back that we love.

Who's with me?[1]

This was the impetus, the inciting incident, the spark.
My sadness, my frustration, my pain.

You will hear me say it several times on this journey of a book: your greatest purpose is often born from your greatest pain. Such was the case for me. So much so that I blindly opened a Google doc after the above article was published and typed: *Who are you away from the field? What makes your heart beat faster?*

These questions would spring an idea. The idea to help others see that there is a king or queen, royalty, inside all of us. That idea became the spark that transformed the pain I was experiencing into a passion that burned bright. That simple idea grew into my life's purpose. And so a movement was born; I just didn't know it yet. It was cellular still, only palpable because of the pain in my gut. It had no name. I just knew I needed to speak my truth.

And speak I did.

I was invited to speak at Florida State University that same August. I spoke on passion and purpose and grabbing the headlines for good things. I spoke about changing the narrative and my own experience with domestic violence. I didn't know what was going to happen or what it would look like beyond that talk. I was just going where the Lord sent me.

Since those early years, the movement has definitely proven ever-evolving. We grew, word spread, people were helped, and we even embraced a name.

#ImChangingtheNarrative

And like the little engine that could, we just kept going. We have now worked with more than sixty colleges and counting and with the Customs and Border Protection, partnered with the Northern Sun and Big 12 sports conferences, and consulted with the Big Ten. We've been featured in international newspapers and even on a giant promo in Times Square. A movement that started with athletes in mind now also inspires CEOs, stay-at-home moms, students, and everyday folks.

Today, our mission statement is "to promote positive mental health and GOOD love for yourself and others by inspiring students, professionals, and parents to create an individual legacy of purpose, passion, and platform." Every book I read, every person I meet, and every life changed along the way puts a log on the fire of my soul and allows me to teach from a place so authentic yet still so raw, but that rawness has an intrinsically powerful edge. It invites any soul that is even minimally conscious and curious to a life of more, a life of different, of better, of non–status quo.

And it all started with an idea.

I wonder what answers you might have if you asked yourself the same two questions. (Just substitute the word "field" for your personal title.) What sort of change could you accomplish in our world? What sorts of movements are lying dormant beneath heaps of pain, just waiting for a spark to ignite them? What might you be able to accomplish if you not only *understood* your own royalty but also *believed* it? Like really believed it.

What sorts of movements are lying dormant beneath heaps of pain, just waiting for a spark to ignite them?

I find that because of what I like to call "funky junk," so many of us never quite understand the majesty within. Funky junk can be anger, bitterness, unforgiveness, mental illness, trauma, abuse, self-loathing, and so much more. These things distract, stand in the way, and steal our joy. But if we put in the time and effort to work through our junk and ultimately let it go, we can start to see ourselves and others clearly. We can see that we were born not just to simply exist or make it through; we were born to leave a legacy! We were born for wholeness and greatness and relentless joy.

When we grab our shovel and do the hard work to get there—things like taking care of our mental health, learning self-care (what we commonly refer to as soul care around the movement), reconciling interpersonal relationships, and discovering our purpose, passion, and platform—we not only heal and grow ourselves but also are able to throw the rope back for someone else so they, too, can be all they were meant to be.

As another anniversary of the movement fast approaches, I finally feel like I can look back and truly marvel at all we created without letting the foot off the proverbial gas. I've had some amazing people helping me on this journey. Some stayed awhile and others were there only for a season, but they know who they are, and #Im ChangingtheNarrative would not be where we are without them.

Because here's the whole truth and nothing but the truth: I have fallen, failed, been broken more times than I can remember, lost everything, and probably turned some people off with my relentless nature; I have been facedown on the floor, and almost took my own life even, but I'm still here! I'm still standing! Thanks in large part to those who loved me even when I didn't love me. And those times I fell and failed, oh boy, did I get up with a vengeance that I'm sure reverberated through the halls of hell. "Oh shoot, that didn't kill her? That didn't steal her joy? Back to the drawing board, guys." I like to think that is the conversation going on in hell every time we crawl back from things that were certainly designed to take us out.

With the help of God and others, I've crawled back from losing everything and kept my joy in the process. And now I get to be that source of support for others (and hopefully you).

I am able to help others because I've been there. While I'm a glass-half-full girl (or as my mom used to call me, the eternal optimist), I can also tell you about life on both sides of the coin—joy and despair. When you are examining yourself, I hope you examine both sides of the coin too. There is great value in knowing yourself, my dear. There is also great value in knowing your pain, what ails you, haunts you, and keeps you pinned down. And there is even more value in deeply loving yourself, but we will get into that throughout this book.

When you are willing to embrace both your strengths and your pain, you are able to help those who are where you have been. I've gotten middle-of-the-night suicide phone calls from people I've spoken to and gotten them professional help. They are all alive and thriving today. I can do that because I've been the one on the other side of the phone in need of a friend.

One of those people I got a call from in the middle of the night now coaches high school football as an assistant coach. We keep in touch from time to time, as is often the case with many of the people I have talked to. I offered to speak to his team via Zoom, and I recently visited with them virtually. When I hung up the Zoom call, I was in a puddle of tears. The enormity of what had just happened enveloped me.

Here was a player I initially spoke to FIVE YEARS AGO! When he called me late one evening, desperate, I had not spoken to him in TWO YEARS! But still, he reached out to me. Why me I'll never know, but I thank God profusely that he thought of me during such a low moment. We, alongside our resident psychologist, Dr. Josh Klapow, got him the immediate help he needed that night, but we also continued to encourage him and check in on him. Fast-forward, he is now thriving and living his best life, and because of him, I got to pour into his players, another generation, another group of souls. Each someone's child. Someone's grandchild. Someone's everything.

And so, the ripple on the pond gets larger.

I've been blessed to have inspired countless people with that same relentless nature that others have always been turned off by. Different strokes for different folks, my people. I've created a movement from zilch, nada, nothing. I created it because I saw a problem and knew I could do something about it.

I say this not to brag but to show you that you can make a difference too!

What issue touches a nerve for you? What problem makes you want to live your life to help others? Haven't some of the greatest things grown from a problem? Sara Blakely created Spanx because women desperately needed better shape and support wear. Lewis Lattimer and Thomas Edison brought us mainstream electricity because they were tired of relying on candlelight night after night.

Let me share an important truth with you: you will die (duh), but your ripple will live on. You may never know who (or how) you affected others in this life with your sheer life force, your smile, and your generosity. Don't ever let anyone talk you out of making an impact, of living with joy, of sharing random compliments with complete strangers. (I'll chase someone down just to tell them something great about themselves.)

That money you left the maid as you departed the hotel or the big honking tip you left at the restaurant when you sensed someone was clearly struggling might be the action that turns everything around for them; it might be *the sign* that restores their faith in humanity. What if that act of generosity was the one they needed to make rent or get a hotel for the night? What if that dollar was the reason they began to hope and believe again for a better future?

If you feel the ping in your soul to turn around and do something for someone, don't you dare let anyone else talk you out of it, even if that person is you. These small acts of kindness begin to train our hearts toward a lifestyle of caring for others.

And that sort of kindness is contagious!

One time, I started picking up trash after a Widespread Panic show in the early days of Bonnaroo. I was tickled pink to slowly see others around me start to grab garbage bags and pick up trash too. Before we knew it, the field was clean and our hearts were happy.

Don't let anyone steer you from the path you know you're supposed to walk (and skip. When is the last time you skipped like a child? I highly recommend it!). If you've lost your way, this book is the invitation to walk (or crawl) back.

I really love this thought that has been attributed to both Carl W. Buehner and Maya Angelou: "I've learned that people will forget what you said, people will forget what you did, but people will never forget how you made them feel."

Right now, in this moment, I want you to lean into their words and remember the people who made you feel worthy, mighty, royal, validated, and seen. Let's take a moment to celebrate them.

The late Cecil Hurt was a legendary reporter for the *Tuscaloosa News*. He interviewed Bear Bryant and Nick Saban and many others in between. He was a giant and genius in the sports reporting world. He was also my friend.

I took the #ImChangingtheNarrative message to University of Alabama football in 2017. I was over-the-moon happy. Alabama is the college football mecca. Working with them will put you on the map in terms of speaking. It was even sweeter because I used to call Tuscaloosa home. I survived a tornado there while huddling in my closet with my two dogs, saying what I thought could be my last words to God. I met my best friend there and became the godmama to her kids. I started a Zumba program there and a prayer circle afterward. I met a precious man named Mr. May there, whom I adopted as my grandfather. I became a better reporter for having covered Nick Saban and Alabama football in Tuscaloosa. And I met Cecil there and cohosted his show for the *Tuscaloosa News*.

He was not able to attend my talk with Alabama football that day in 2017 but called me right after. This normally curmudgeonesque, even stodgy, man said, "You don't get it, do you?"

"Get what?" I asked.

"You think you're solely affecting players in that room, Rachel, but if one player goes back and breaks the generational cycle of poverty, drugs, or substance abuse, if one player changes the narrative in his family, in any way, or changes the way he deals with and talks about his mental health, then it affects his grandkids, and so on and so forth. It's not just the players you spoke to today, Rachel. It's so much bigger than that."

Wooo, boy, that's the good stuff right there!

I can close my eyes and still reach out and touch the dashboard of the car I was sitting in when he said that. I can even see the foliage and the restaurant I was sitting in front of.

Sidenote: I am working on genuinely receiving compliments. In my past, for a myriad of reasons, they have made me uncomfortable. I would dig my nails into my hands and deflect with another genuine compliment to the giver, never letting the words pierce the deepest veil of my soul. But on that day, I felt his words. They blew open a hole in my soul of knowing what I was truly created for, a chasm so wide I could never go back. I could never not do this work. Someone's grandchild could be changed because of it. And they were depending on me to use my pain for a purpose.

And there is this: for all the pain I've experienced, there's still more joy than I can count. And oh, the life change that has happened because I've chosen to use my pain for purpose and count my joy instead of my pain.

It really comes down to a simple question, my love: Are you a victim or a victor? That is a decision we all get to make and it is made in our minds, hearts, and souls.

What follows in the chapters to come is a collection of stories that pack a punch. After all, my movement is built on my stories and the art of storytelling. These are tales that will immediately put you at the center of the action, narratives that will bind up and break your heart at the same time.

One of the greatest compliments I have ever received was from the head coach of East Carolina University at the time, Scottie Montgomery, who said, "It works so well [your talks] because it's your life. It's your story. You're not coming in and trying to tell someone else's story. You don't talk down to them. You lift them up. You infuse hope into them. That's why you are so effective."

And that's my hope for this book. So buckle up. I'm going to share with you some of the most impactful moments of my life, the ones that shaped and molded me into who I am. I am also going to share my heartbreaking failures and the times I summited the mountaintop. My hope? That you can see shades of yourself in my missives. That you will travel to Israel and Africa with me on the wings of my memories. That my tales will push you, grow you, challenge you, and ultimately change you.

I sometimes wonder what would have happened if I had never answered the call of my soul, the call to create this movement. And

I wonder who I would be and where I would be. I'm fairly certain I would be successful, but I know beyond a shadow of a doubt that I would be far emptier for never having fully put my finger on what it was that was missing. I'm sure I'd feel a real and palpable ache for what could've been. I don't stay in that imaginary place long because it's too painful for me.

I am walking in all my glory now, and I can't imagine any other life.

I want the same for you.

You may not know just yet what the question is that will spark *your* passion. That's okay. The only thing required of you as we take this journey together is an open heart and mind. I'm going to touch places in your heart that might sting a little. This is not because I hate you but because our pain and triggers are often surprising and beautiful invitations to healing. The ride will be bumpy and tumultuous, but boy, will it be worth it if you are willing to punch your ticket. I can't wait to see who you become and what you accomplish.

I am now a soul on fire, but because I was once a burning building myself, it is imprinted on my DNA to carry buckets of water for people who are still burning buildings themselves. My mission? To go back and show you how to find the embers of passion hidden in the ashes. I have a message of hope, truth, and purpose, and I'm giving it to you. In the end, I hope you'll carry the water with me— for yourself and others.

The journey has begun, and here is your first joystart! Go ahead and mark up the margins of this book or write in the journaling space included in the back of this book. (Truthfully, I hope you come back to these very notes many times over.) You might have a question or thought that has been pinging around in your head and heart for many moons now. Listen to me, don't tamp it out or ignore it any longer. It is bouncing around your head for a reason.

Are you ready? Let's go!

JOYSTART

When considering your life, actions, and inner dialogue, what stories do you tell yourself and what stories do you tell the world around you? I want you to sit down and ponder on this one. Are they negative, depressing stories of brokenness, or are you telling stories of hope, joy, peace, and overcoming?

I want to tell stories of overcoming, stories of finding joy in the midst of immense pain, and stories that will inspire people for generations to come. I want to teach you to tell similar stories, my friend. Make them good ones. You and I are literally writing the book of our lives at this very moment. And one day, that will be all that's left of us—our stories, our legacy, and our (good) name. Jesus once said, "A good man brings good things out of the good stored up in his heart, and an evil man brings evil things out of the evil stored up in his heart. For the mouth speaks what the heart is full of" (Luke 6:45).

What is your heart full of, beloved? That is what I hope you will investigate in the coming days as we walk through this journey together!

Once you have journaled some about the stories you are telling, write one sentence or question that is burning in your heart right now. What truth would you write in response to that sentence or question at this moment? Here are a few questions you might consider:

What am I created for?

Who am I outside of being a mom or a dad? (I've gotten this one recently.)

Who am I away from my career?

What is my legacy?

What brings me joy?

How can I cultivate joy on a daily basis?

What would a healing version of me look like?

CHAPTER 2

People First

From a young age, I can remember my mom caring deeply about people, people she didn't even know. I remember distinctly the smell of blueberry muffins coming from the kitchen on Saturday mornings. They were off-limits to the family. My mom and I would bag them up, all pretty, without me tasting even one, and off we went. Our destination was a nearby nursing home. We visited and gave out the big, honking blueberry muffins to people who hadn't had visitors in the longest time.

I remember my mom asking the nurse at the front desk, "Who gets visitors the least? Who has been alone the longest?"

The sweet nurses would take us to those folks. We not only gave them the muffins; we also sat with them. We visited and loved on them. Jesus calls those who are the most neglected and forgotten in our world *the least of these*: "The King will reply, 'Truly I tell you, whatever you did for one of the least of these brothers and sisters of mine, you did for me'" (Matt. 25:40).

Turns out that our presence was a far greater gift than the muffins. I just didn't get that yet because I wasn't fully formed—and I really wanted those muffins. But what I did understand was how the people came alive at the sight of a mother and daughter together, united, a duo, a team, especially one that wanted to stay awhile and visit.

After our visit, once back in the car, my mom would pull one last big, honking blueberry muffin from her bag—one that was previously hidden—and ceremoniously give it to me. I would have blueberries smeared clear across my face on the way home. I was that giddy. But more than that my heart was full, and my love tank was officially at overflow. She had shown me the greatest, most magnanimous gift, the gift of giving, the gift of loving people you don't know from Adam's house cat (an old Southern saying that originated from the phrase "not to know one from Adam's off ox," meaning the person is a total stranger). As you can imagine, this left an incredible impression on me as an eleven-year-old.

People often ask me, "Why are you the way you are? You seem very happy."

I can point back to those blueberry muffins and our trips to the local nursing home as one giant reason why. Because of those trips, I learned to value people and derive joy from simple interactions with other human beings.

My mom also raised me on the author Og Mandino. He had a big influence on how my mom treated others. We had Og's books all around our house. The covers were worn and well-loved. (Sidenote: I think books well-worn by love are right up there with pretty vistas, gorgeous natural wonders, and great works of art. Am I right or am I right?)

If you've never heard of Og, let me give you a quick lesson, straight from the man himself:

> Beginning today, treat everyone you meet as if they were going to be dead by midnight. Extend to them all the care, kindness and understanding you can muster, and do it with no thought of any reward. Your life will never be the same again.[1]

Powerful stuff, huh?

This is the start of relentless joy. Everything I will teach you in this book is built on this simple principle: the most joy-filled life is lived with others in mind. In this life as you start to look outside of yourself, you will begin to see people as miracles, experiences as miracles, and nature as miraculous. Once applied, it will totally transform the way you interact with people on a soul level.

Og Mandino understood this, but he knew heartbreak too. Born in 1923, he was set to attend Missouri Journalism School after high school, but then his mother dropped dead from a heart attack while she was making him lunch. Instead, he went to work in a factory and then, in WWII, served as a bombardier and flew thirty missions over Germany. When he returned, he had a hard time finding work, so he became a traveling insurance salesman. Lonely nights away from family and spent in bars led to alcoholism, and soon Og couldn't hold down a job. He lost his wife and family during the course of these events.

One wintry night, he almost took his own life, but instead he went to his local library and read every book he could get his hands on. He would follow this visit with many more stops at libraries all over this great land, reading every book on successful people he could. This new focus helped Og to eventually turn his life around. He overcame his alcoholism, became a skilled salesman, and even started writing pamphlets to help others in business and life—a path that would lead him to become an international multibestseller and renowned speaker. His books are built on the principle that you and everyone else hold extraordinary value.[2]

And this is how Og made an impression on one woman (my mom), who then raised her daughter (me) to believe those same things about people. (I think it's important to note that my daddycakes did good deeds too. I just didn't know about most of them until after he died. More on my precious papa later.)

One of my life's mottos is "Relationships are my currency, therefore I'm a billionaire." I don't count my wealth monetarily; I count it through the richness of people that I love and that love me. My tapestry of wealth (relationships) is bold, diverse, young, old, wise, silly, crazy, calm, smart, all of the above, and more.

I am beyond blessed.

What does your tapestry look like? What and who make up its beauty? If your tapestry isn't what you want it to be, I challenge you to implement Og's words daily, and see how it grows. Could you seek to deepen the relationships around you, be they at work, home, or in your community? Could you be a "no-

What does your tapestry look like? What and who make up its beauty?

ticer" who seeks to see all the good already in the people around you? Because here's the truth: there are people in my tapestry who aren't family, they aren't close friends, but you bet they have come into my life and made a mark. Some were in and out of my life in minutes, some hours, and others days, but nevertheless, their thread is bright and strong in my tapestry.

And did you know that from a psychological standpoint you do leave a mark on people and can change the way they feel, in a literal sense?

Two psychologists, Noah Eisenkraft and Hillary Anger Elfenbein, asked themselves in 2010 whether it was possible for some people to emanate a special emotional influence that made others feel safe and at ease or, the opposite, feel discomfort.

In one of their studies, they assigned 239 college students of different nationalities to different groups of four or five members. They then enrolled them in the same class for a semester and asked them to do a project together. Each member of the group would eventually evaluate how the rest of their classmates made them feel. They took into account eight different emotions: stressed, bored, angry, sad, calm, relaxed, happy, and enthusiastic.

The two researchers found that some people almost always affected others in the same way, regardless of their mood and who they were affecting. They indicated that "there are significant differences in how people experience their emotions and the influence that those emotions exert on the others."[3] In other words, beyond how we personally feel, our emotions influence the people around us. This is called "affective presence":

> The affective presence is an effect that we produce in others without realizing it, a kind of 'affective vibration' that has the same result on everybody we relate with, making them feel good or bad, regardless of their previous mood. . . .
>
> Like the rest of personality traits, some people have a more marked affective presence than others. There are people who make us feel comfortable quickly and transmit their vitality and joy, while the contact with others is more affectively flat and we need more time to capture their affective presence.[4]

What I found remarkable is the fact that people with a strong affective presence don't always feel joy or zest themselves. Maybe they have had a difficult life or suffered a psychological trauma, yet they are still able to produce a great sense of calm or pass on a lot of enthusiasm.

That's the kind of person I want to be, the kind that can soften the noise in my own life so that others are not affected. That doesn't mean I don't feel my feelings or take time to process them. It just means I strive not to let my range and flow of emotions affect everyone around me. Instead, I want my presence to instill joy in those around me, even when I am having a hard day or feeling down. That's what it means to be a joystarter! I don't know if I'll ever completely get there, but it's a beautiful, faraway mountaintop that I'll forever try to summit.

I once heard a friend say, "I want to be a Bible with skin on it. Will I ever achieve that? Heck no. But I will keep trying." I love her words. They have never left me. (Thanks, Keyshonda!) They remind me of this verse: "In the same way, let your light shine before others, that they may see your good deeds and glorify your Father in heaven" (Matt. 5:16).

There are some people who just feel like light. I want to be one of those people until I take my last breath on this planet. You or I might be the only Jesus someone ever sees (us as a reflection of Him). They may never have stepped foot in a church or owned a Bible. Or maybe they've been church-hurt or people-hurt (or shamed), so they have their walls up, their defenses thick as steel. If we are the only Jesus they ever see, then I want them to see Him for who He truly is: a loving, joyful, doting, passionate Abba Father.

My friend Samantha used to work for a nursing home company. One day she picked me up in her convertible and off we went to buy every flower and stuffed animal from the grocery store. We literally bought them out, boxes of them! She picked one of her nursing homes and we delivered those flowers and stuffed animals with the greatest of love. Samantha gets people. She deals in an eternal currency.

That day was one of the best days of my life. Afterward, the wind whipped through my hair in that convertible, and purpose coursed through my veins. It was a heck of a feeling (looking back, it is one that I desperately wish I could have bottled for harder days—because they were coming). The faces of those residents as they received their unexpected gifts are forever etched in my mind. And for a second, those flowers could've been big, honking blueberry muffins. I was instantly transported back to my childhood. I was eleven all over again and visiting a nursing home with my mommy. I got to spend time with little Rachel for a moment in time and give her a soul hug. And I got to see my beautiful mommy through my childhood eyes.

That's the good stuff. The healing stuff.

I love Proverb 3:27 because it reminds me that I have the power to do good for others every day:

> Do not withhold good from those to whom it is due,
>   when it is in your power to act.

Yes, I have felt joy when *I* accomplished something amazing or when something good happened for or to *me*. But there is a special level of joy when, from the purest part of your soul, you do good for *others*. I bet you would agree!

My friend Dr. Kevin Elko likes to say, "Don't pray for a blessing; pray to be a blessing." That's the best kind of joy, the kind that has nothing to do with you other than you being the conduit.

That's relentless joy!

I once met a king in Austin, Texas. (We are all kings and queens, you know; some of us just need to discover this truth inside of us, and some of us still need to do the work to forgive ourselves and others and then walk in that sweet knowing.) He happened to be driving my Uber. I was in town to see LSU football take on the University of Texas Longhorns in one of the most anticipated games of the young season. LSU is one of my #ImChangingtheNarrative teams, and I was there to support them as they took on this vaunted opponent. I got a ride from the airport, and on the way to my hotel, I wanted to spoil myself. My guilty pleasure is the chicken crisper meal at Chili's. I love the honey mustard, and don't even get me started on the corn on the cob. It's *slap yo mama* good!

I called an Uber to take me from Chili's to my hotel, and a nice black vehicle awaited me outside. The driver's name was Lawrence. In the short six-minute ride, he poured life into me. It was like he knew right where the gas tank of my existence was located. We bonded instantly on such a deep level. He shared with me about a particular ride. He had picked up a man who had just been released from a correctional facility. He poured into that young man the same way he was pouring into me on my ride. REAL-LIFE talk! That young man would later share that on the day King Lawrence picked him up, he was on his way home to end his life. He credits King Lawrence as the reason he did not.

I was so moved that I gave King Lawrence my card and a bracelet, normally reserved for athletes and coaches, that had #ImChanging theNarrative embossed across it. I got out of the car, absolutely gobsmacked, and hugged him with a farewell message. "Keep being a king!" I said. That ride and our convo meant so much to me. I thought that was the last time I would ever see this real-life angel.

So you can imagine my sheer shock when I called an Uber again for a ride to the airport after the game, and there to pick me up was King Lawrence. (By the way, he goes by Lawrence. But by this point, I had dubbed him King Lawrence.) I got into the car in near tears. He said he had prayed that he might get to drive me again, but y'all, this is Austin. It isn't a small town. The odds of being paired again with Lawrence were slim to none—and slim left town.

It was miraculous to see his kind face again. We had church in that car the entire way to the airport. Happy tears—as my precious soulmate of a grandmother called them—streamed down my face the entire way to the airport. And if that wasn't enough, he told me some of his passengers that weekend had seen my bracelet on his arm and he apparently went on and on about me and #ImChanging theNarrative. To this day, I still keep up with King Lawrence. He was, and is, living proof that if you put people first, you will continually be blessed and live this life in complete awe and wonder at what might happen next.

I'm not naive to what some of you might be thinking as you read this right now: *Well, Rachel, it's just not that easy for me. I don't often encounter Samanthas or Lawrences. I run into people who are salty, mean, combative, angry, or downright nasty. I'm talking people who make it hard to be kind.*

I've met those people too. Heck, I've been one of those folks myself! When I have these encounters, I find they go one of two ways. I meet their displeasure with displeasure and then I end up feeling terrible afterward because now we are both miserable, and on top of it, I'm ashamed of myself for being miserable back. Or I meet their displeasure, their hurt, their loneliness, their shame, their grief, their disdain, their anger with love.

Love is the only antidote that ever solves a thing. Love. Sweet love. It has the power to break the cycle of pain and hurt. Recently, I met a woman who was wound tightly and closed up like a school building on the weekends. But once she felt the genuine care I showed for who she was as a person, I watched her start to open up like a flower receiving the sun at first dew. Now listen, if that sounds hokey, that's okay. I'm sort of hokey, but I'm on a different plane in terms of living. Your invitation is embossed and ready. I want you to join me here.

I have witnessed this metamorphosis with my own two eyes, and more importantly, I have felt it in my soul, again and again. It's the good stuff of life. Better than a million-dollar deposit into the bank is playing a part in a soul coming back to life!

And might I add that Jesus genuinely cared for people, even those who didn't deserve his love. He dined with ladies of the night and tax collectors, called some of the worst sinners to follow him, and told a thief on a cross next to him that he would be with him that day in paradise. He broke the cycle of shame and wounding with radical love.

The Bible says, "But God showed his great love for us by sending Christ to die for us *while we were still sinners*" (Rom. 5:8 NLT, emphasis mine). He doesn't wait for us to be good people or in the right mood. He doesn't need us to be perfectly religious first. He meets us with love *where we are*.

And Jesus is the most joy-filled person there has ever been—and the greatest joystarter of all time. The world doesn't need more religion; it desperately needs more people who genuinely care about others like Jesus did and does.

JOYSTART

Spend some time thinking about your affective presence. How do you think you make others around you feel most of the time? It might be a tough question to ask yourself, but we did say this would be hard work. Write it down, good or bad. Think through how you might hone and strengthen your affective presence for the better.

Some ways that I have found to do this are through various reminders. Write out reminders of the above Og principle and put them in places you will interact with during your day such as a sticky note on your mirror. Put a folded napkin or a slip of paper in the crevice of your steering wheel to remind you when you're in traffic not to flip someone off (real talk). This note on the steering wheel was a favorite of my mom's when she needed to remember something. It would jog her memory before, during, and after her drive.

I also love the reminder app on my phone. I will set it to remind me of things today, next week, and next year. It is literally how I survive. I love checking things off this digital list as much as I do actually accomplishing the thing itself. Can you feel me? There is great satisfaction in that. In fact, I've remade lists just to scratch them off! I know, I know. This is borderline insanity, but it's how I'm wired, and I'm okay with that. As I mentioned, laughing at myself is a huge key to my preservation. And I keep myself in stitches.

There's one last profound way of remembering these principles and other things: ask God to help you. I was taking a walk in my neighborhood when I lived in Atlanta a few years back. I remember my anxiety starting to ramp up because I couldn't remember something I was supposed to do, something that had never made it onto a list or a calendar. As I was working myself up into a big fit, with thoughts racing through my head, I heard the voice, the good one, the reassuring one: "Trust me. Give it to me. I will help you remember."

I stopped dead in my tracks and looked up. That was a God shot, a God wink, and I was grateful. Ever since that moment, when I begin to get spun up, I remember those words.

I simply utter, "Help me, God."

I cannot count the times when whatever it was I was forgetting came to me through a song, something I was reading, or a person, but it almost always came back. And when it didn't, the world didn't stop revolving. I can assure you of that. I learned from it and got better. A mistake isn't a failure unless you don't learn from it, chil'! And when we struggle to remember to love others throughout our day, we can ask God for help there too.

CHAPTER 3

On a Hill in Africa

Jambo, jambo, wakey, wakey.... Coffee or tea?"

That greeting woke me every morning on safari in Kenya. On this particular day, I was waking up in a home that formerly belonged to famed war correspondent Martha Gellhorn, who was once married to Ernest Hemingway. No biggie. (Who am I kidding? I am a history nerd, so that fact just bedazzled my nerdy little soul.)

I dressed hurriedly to get out to the veranda. An unforgettable sight awaited. As the sun rose in all its glory, it revealed endless rolling hills dotted with zebras and giraffes. The house sat on a hill overlooking this gorgeous scene. As if it couldn't get any better, someone had brought an old-timey record player onto the grassy area just in front of the house, and the soundtrack from *Out of Africa* was playing. If you've never seen the film, I highly recommend it for the acting, the scenery, the true love story, and the music—HOLY COW—the music. It will stir up something deep inside of you, and it will do it in a hurry. (And Robert Redford is easy on the eyes too. Just saying.) Lickety-split, you'll be looking for your passport to go to Africa.

This was my own real-life African adventure. I was there (in part) because some poor soul backed out of the safari my aunt Karen helped to organize just a tad too late to get their deposit back. (Whoever you are, thank you!) I had been on the air in Columbus, Georgia, hosting a sports talk show when my aunt called.

"Would you like to go on a safari?"

"Ummm yes, would I?" I replied. "But a young, broke professional cannot afford a dream trip like this, nor can I take the two weeks off."

"It's free," she said. "All you need is to get your passport and anti-malaria meds."

"You had me at *it's free*, Aunt K."

So here I was in Africa, and let me tell you, there is nothing like an African night sky. The stars are so bright and seem so close that you feel like you could reach up and grab them. (I like to imagine that in heaven those same stars will be in reach, that we will literally be able to touch them. Can you even imagine?) If I let my mind go back, I can even conjure up the smell of the African Serengeti. I can smell the dirt and the mud and the clay and the animal dung. And the birds are so colorful and look like something out of your imagination.

There is a tree called an acacia tree that looks like it is covered in toothpicks. And the tree of life that resides over Disney's Animal Kingdom is called a baobab tree. It is composed of 76 percent water. In more arid regions, people often cut hollows in baobabs to create storage wells to catch rainwater as the trees store water in natural hollows between branches and on the outside of the trunk. Pretty neat, huh?

When people ask me about my time in Kenya, I describe it like this: Imagine you're at the zoo. The animals are in a cage, and you're free to peer in at them. In the wild parts of Africa, you're in the cage—the car, that is—and they are free. They peer at you if you're lucky. I have driven up to the lip of a prehistoric volcano and then dipped down into it to watch a cape buffalo harass a male lion . . .

and WIN! I have climbed out on top of a jeep parked in a savannah in the midst of a herd of elephants we had been searching for days to find. We were in absolute wonder and sitting very still because any sudden movements or noise could cause them to trample the car. (It was also at this moment that I discovered the real need for and importance of green, tan, neutral, safari-colored clothes, which somehow I had forgotten to gather in my hasty packing. Bad Rachel, bad. Fashion is not necessary for a safari.)

We were also fortunate to see a mother cheetah teaching her adolescent cubs how to hunt and giving chase to a gazelle that lived to see another day. I'll never forget the guide telling us how rare this sighting was. I distinctly remember scribbling in my journal that I had just gone to church and saw Jesus in that encounter. And this was only topped by being in one of our camps toward the end of the safari and seeing two very endangered and near-extinct male rhinos fighting nearby. We all watched, quite ready to spring an escape but unable to take our eyes off the sight. This is the kind of stuff I think we will see in heaven—minus the fighting. So it'll just be two male rhinos being friends.

Still a sight to behold.

I have to admit, I did not think I was going to make it back from Africa. You see, one of our "fun" excursions was getting into canoes and leisurely floating on a lake chock-full of hippos. In case you, like me, weren't aware, hippos are quite a tempestuous bunch. They have incisors sometimes a foot long and, though herbivores, will also take you to the bottom of a river or lake, spin you, drown you, bite you in half, and then just leave you because—ya know—they like plants. They actually kill and harm more people in Africa than any other large animal, carnivore or otherwise, and can run up to twenty miles per hour!

So there we were, on a lake full of hippos, ON PURPOSE! I was literally hyperventilating. I had joked to my mother before leaving, "American Killed by Hippo" would be the headline. I was surely going to die on this excursion. And the hilarious part is that everyone else was quite unaffected. I looked back at the guide/driver as he picked up a very large stick and went about beating it on the bottom of the canoe.

"What's that for," I asked.

He replied, "To scare hippos away, so they don't capsize us."

Dear sweet baby Jesus. I have never thanked God more than when we headed for shore and my feet touched the dock.

That is the wonder and terror of the bush in Africa, particularly Kenya. It is that wild. That big. That in your face with no regard for feelings or comfort. The wild of Africa is raw and rare and if you should ever have the chance, you must go.

Back on the veranda at Martha Gellhorn's house, I sipped my coffee and looked over the grassy knoll, gobsmacked. I couldn't help but look up and thank GOD over and over and over again. Not only was the view awe-inspiring but so was the real-life heroine, who many moons ago woke up to this stunning view daily and likely stood in the exact same spot as I was.

A famous war correspondent, Martha Gellhorn traveled to war zones and covered conflicts for sixty years. She covered virtually every conflict of the twentieth century and was the only woman to stand on the beaches of Normandy on D-Day. That's insane if you stop to think of it. She was drawn to the victims of war more than to the generals or the heads of state. While others were drawn to the powerful, she was seemingly drawn to the broken, the affected, and the oppressed.

Woo-wee, that will preach.

Her propensity for the seemingly peculiar didn't stop there either. She had dropped out of college because she was bored as a student (a lot of us can relate), moved to Paris, and started a journalism career at Hearst publications. In 1934 she returned to the United States where she got a job working for the head of FEMA. Talk about falling forward!

During WWII, Martha ignored military restrictions on female war correspondents and stowed away on a hospital ship to get a firsthand account of the Allied invasion of France in 1944. She reported from the beaches of Normandy in a nurse's uniform. (What a gutsy chick!) According to many historians, she apparently never knew if she was going to be alive the next day, and that was immensely interesting to her.

When the war ended, Martha went with the liberation troops to the Dachau concentration camp, which she called a "circle of hell." She reported, "Behind the wire and the electric fence, the skeletons sat in the sun and scratched themselves for lice. They have no age and no faces; they all look alike and like nothing you will ever see if you are lucky."[1]

I think back now and wonder how she rectified the polarity of her experiences: to see death and destruction in such an intimate way, etched on the faces and in the sunken eye sockets of strangers at Dachau, and then to stand here and witness the majesty, the beauty of the African plains. How could she reconcile the two?

I thought I was going for a safari. Instead, a gutsy war correspondent reached across history to challenge me to look at the dichotomy of joy and pain in my own life.

You and I may not have seen the faces at Dachau or a city ravaged after a war, but if we look at our own lives, I'm sure there are parts that feel blasted, barren, or left for dead. Maybe you never got to have a baby after watching others bring life into the world with ease. Maybe past abuse has left you with hidden scars that you fear may never heal. Maybe you have seen so much death around you that you feel like you're fighting your own personal war. (I know I do.) Maybe you're still mourning all you were "supposed" to achieve but did not.

I get it. I do. It's a battle that is quite familiar to me. I know when I get to heaven, God is surely going to say, "You sure kept me busy asking me 'Why?' all the time."

When I examine my past, I can remember snippets of joy, even at the worst times. Days after my mama passed away, I spontaneously pulled over to have a selfie session in a field of wildflowers. I had always wanted to do it but had never gotten the chance. That moment in time in that field of beauty made my pain less raw; it held it at bay for a minute. It greased the edges, if you will. Maybe joy is a lubricant, a buffer.

Maybe joy is the emotion that most "has our back."

Let me explain. Have you ever been heartbroken but still able to find happiness in the laughter of a child? That is persistent joy. Hit rock bottom financially and someone shows you a grand act of generosity? That's joy showing up in the lurch. Did someone drop off a care package while you were sick or come sit with you when you lost a loved one? That's joy in times of suffering. That's joy that has our back!

I wonder, if you take a gander back at your history, where would joy be hidden in your story? I'd be willing to bet that it was present, having your back, even at the worst of times. When we are looking for it, joy will nudge us at just the right time. Obey the nudge.

When we are looking for it, joy will nudge us at just the right time. Obey the nudge.

It's kind of like rainbows or redbirds. I'm serious. The last one you saw was a love note just for you. Redbirds were always my family's thing. They still are. We believe the old lore that when you see one, you are seeing a visitor from heaven. At some of the most important times in my life, there has mysteriously been a redbird. And when I've been the most broken, one would appear—one time literally flapping furiously outside my passenger window as I sped onto the freeway. I was going sixty miles per hour, so that redbird was persistent! That bird—that joy chasing me with reckless abandon—was a message for me. A reminder that God would see me through. I know it like I know the sun will come up tomorrow.

Now, I am well aware that life isn't full of love notes for a lot of people. But joy isn't like the fleeting happiness that the world peddles. Real, relentless joy is more like a love story. Despite the ups and downs, joy never fails. It is always seeking you, knows you, wants to cushion your falls and bring a smile to your beautiful face. That's love and that's *real* joy. I think sometimes pain becomes so normal in our lives that we miss out on the joy that has been put before us. This book is your invitation, from this moment forward, to never miss the opportunity to savor the joy in your life.

If you did an audit on the worst times of your life, and got down to the granular details, I'm willing to bet there was something beautiful even in the midst of that pain.

I can count all I've lost, and it is a lot, or I can count my joy. The choice is up to me.

I know this, Martha went to Africa after Dachau. She built a lodge high atop a hill in Kenya for solitude, and to write, according to her own memoirs. I like to think she was searching for joy after all the pain she saw covering wars for so many years. Maybe her soul needed to feel goodness again, in all its purity and simplicity.

I think it's important to remind you that in no way am I advocating you run from your pain. In fact, I'm championing you to sit with it on your proverbial hill in Africa—your own place of peace where you can feel deeply and experience the unshakable joy that was always there, the joy that is just waiting to be embraced, waiting to walk with you toward healing.

I hope that this book can help you to create a place like that inside yourself. A place secure enough that it can experience both the pains and joys of your story—where you can pause, breathe, and feel again.

If we let it, death, destruction, and depression will back us into a dark and desolate corner. I know this to be true in my own life. I also know the tiniest step forward—crawling counts—is so very brave. Maybe for Martha, Africa was her way of crawling out of that dark place. Maybe she stood in the same spot as me and found peace in the rawness and vastness of Africa. Maybe that's how she reconciled all she saw in the many wars she covered and at the liberation of Dachau. I'd love to travel back in time and tell her what a rad chick she was, but living this life, my life, with everything I've got will have to be my ode to Ol' Martha.

How will you reconcile the pain of your life? How will you crawl out of your dark place? Where is your Africa? Martha moved to Africa and built a house in the middle of nowhere. I don't recommend you do this, but I've discovered that oftentimes the greatest pain we experience is tied to our greatest purpose. I long to build my house mentally on a hill in Africa, just like Martha. I am not running from the pain in my life, but I do have to consciously choose, daily, to bust open the windows of the (cozy) home of my soul and let in all the light, all the brilliance, all the majesty that this world can offer.

I could keep the shutters closed. I could focus on all the loss, but like Martha, I don't want to miss the light, the joy, the wildness, and the wonder that life has to offer. Take a note from the mama cheetah I saw while on safari. She can't be passive if she wants to eat. She can't rest on her laurels if she wants to teach her kids to hunt and survive. No, she's on the prowl and puts herself out there—sometimes in harm's way—because she wants herself and her family to live their fullest lives. You should want that for yourself too.

Open the shutters of your soul. Dust off the residue of the past. Be aware. Be on the prowl for joy. Think of Martha. Think of me. And start crawling toward that place of peace where you can feel again. Don't be ashamed if you find that you're still crawling tomorrow or the next day. (Shame ain't welcome around these parts!) Start crawling for your house on a hill in Africa. And when you get there, unlatch the windows with gratitude to let your life light in.

JOYSTART

I promised you takeaways, real-life change, people. So here it is!

Get a piece of paper out and draw a line down the middle. Look back at your life. On one side write everything that has hurt you in the past and in the present. (If you need multiple pieces of paper, that is okay too.)

Get the microscope out. Be willing to go there and feel your pain. Let's be honest with ourselves, joystarters! Go ahead and get it out. Acknowledge it. Sit with it. Let those feelings of hurt, loss, pain, whatever they may be, flow through you. The more we sit with our feelings and hurts, the better we process them and the less scary they are the next go-round.

Now, *on the other side* of the line write every single joy, memory, and blessing you can think of. (Start by writing what is top of mind, but feel free to keep this list going. You can add to it as you remember sweet memories and sweet moments of joy!) I've found that even in the worst times, I could still see joy in the picture. There it was, joy begging to be noticed and indulged in. I bet you can too, if you look hard enough. A special moment with a friend in the middle of a hard time. A good that grew out of difficulty. Whatever you love that is unique to you, that's something you can write down. Saw or experienced something awesome that was just for you? Another thing for the joy list! I'm serious. Those special moments that speak to our hearts are part of the bigger love story from our Papa God to us.

A short sample of my joy list would look something like this:

My faith

My husband

My bonus kids

My family

Loved ones who are my chosen family

My natural gift of encouragement

A roof over my head

The love of my mama and the life we shared together

Being adopted by my daddy and how much he wanted me

Creating the #ImChangingtheNarrative movement

Mentoring and connecting people

Breath in my lungs

My *joy*ful nature

My fur-baby

College football

Golf

Travel and all the memories it brings

When your pain drags you back to a dark place, look at your list and start preaching to yourself. Speak life over yourself, over your circumstances, over your pain.

"I am hurting now, but I'm on the way to being well. I'm healing!"

"I may not be where I want to be financially, but I'm learning, hustling, saving, and setting goals by creating new spending habits."

"I'm not in a great place in my marriage or romantically, but I am working on uncovering my own experiences and trauma and how that affects who I show up as in relationships."

See the difference there? You're acknowledging the pain but also speaking life over yourself. As my mama would say: "No more stinkin' thinkin'."

(Some people I've taught over the years have used sticky notes to attach to their mirror or door to remind them.)

This is how you start to build that house on a hill—by allowing the good and bad in life to commingle and by allowing your memories of joy to soothe you and carry you through the most difficult moments.

CHAPTER 4

Don't Look Away

I knew she wasn't long from heaven. I was watching her take her last ragged and labored breaths on this planet. Her body was slap-worn down from fighting cancer for ten months, maybe more. The doctor told us she had probably had it many, many years before, but it was kept at bay due to her healthy lifestyle choices.

Something happens when you (and your stepdad) have to physically hold up your sweet mama to shower her limp body. Something deeply painful, like it's in your bones. Looking back, I can only attribute that feeling to my whole being wrestling with the idea that I was about to live the rest of my life without my mama.

And every day I would have to swallow that jagged little pill.

My mom and I weren't always so close. It was my grandmother (my mom's mom) that I was the spitting image of. She was my soulmate, my finish-my-sentences person, the pea to my pod, her birthday just days from mine.

No, I hadn't always been close with my mama. It wasn't that I didn't want to be. It was just complicated, as these things often are. Does anyone out there feel me?

She was the child of an alcoholic father. She loved him deeply, despite the abuse. She grew up and repeated the cycle, craving a partner like wooden furniture craves some Old English oil. It wasn't her fault, not by a long shot. She was just a wounded (but exotic) bird (we are Mayan, Mexican, Jewish, English, Peruvian, and Native American). And a strong bird at that. She didn't take a pain pill for nearly all of her ten-month stage-four cancer battle. Only in her last forty-eight hours on this earth did she call for the morphine.

Yep. She was that kind of strong.

After my grandmother died, my mom and I got the most unexpected gift. We became best friends in my abuelita's absence. In her passing, Abuelita passed the baton, and for the next seven years, I got the gift of being best friends with my mama. We began finishing each other's sentences. We leaned in. We sought to forgive harder and understand each other even more. We started a clothing business together, we pushed each other, we yay-yay'd at each other (another way of saying we argued), but not in a malicious way. It was just a mother and daughter speaking a language only they can speak. LOL.

We had nicknames for each other: Booty and Tooty. We took trips and danced when no one was watching—and when everyone was watching. She even became my mom-ager (mom + manager) for a spell, calling on my behalf to close deals since we didn't have the same last name. Forget that we sounded and looked just alike. Our bad. We tried.

We were just that close. Our newfound übercloseness radiated to those around us and on social media. People remarked about our relationship and the beautiful bond we had, that we were the spitting image of each other in our outward appearance, and perhaps even more profound, that our souls were so much alike. People thanked us for inspiring them to call their own mothers, to love harder and to forgive more freely. My mama would friend every friend I had on Facebook and encourage them on her own. That was just her way. (We are both natural encouragers. That's the cloth we are cut from.) And many a time I would go to comment on someone's good news and she had beat me to it, literally taking the words from my heart before I could type them. That was us. We had a special, remarkable kind of love.

When she died, I lost a piece of myself. I wonder if you can relate?

There are days that are harder than others and some moments are just too much to bear. For me, I have found grief best served in releasing myself fully to the anguish of that moment, letting the pain pulsate through my body. Then feebly saying to it, "Please close the door on the way out." But the sad truth is that the door never really closes. It always stays cracked. Grief is not tidy or respectful of our wishes. It's the fire alarm that loses the battery at 3:00 a.m., incessantly showing up at the worst of times with a heart-piercing beep.

On this side of grief though, I am learning some truths that I think might help you. For one, to have lost greatly means you've loved greatly, and if it means giving up that epic kind of love to feel less grief, well that's not a trade-off I'm willing to make.

I bet you're not either.

About four months into her ten-month battle, I got one of the greatest gifts—a piece of wisdom. (BTW, I hope some of your greatest gifts are not earthly things you can touch and hold but bits of wisdom so magnificent they are almost beyond words.)

I was in my local tea shop, High Garden Tea Company in East Nashville, talking to the owner Leah Larabell. She and her husband are educated in the medicine of teas and herbs from all corners of this planet. They also regularly hosted sweat lodges on their magical property with a local Native American medicine man and flute player. Their tea shop looked like something out of *The Hobbit* with herbs hanging from the ceiling, jars lining the walls, and in the back, a homemade kombucha bar. Leah regularly sat with people, listened to their maladies, and offered her suggestion for teas she and her husband had concocted—always with the disclaimer that she was not a doctor and was just giving friendly advice.

Did I mention this place also had a friendly ban on cell phones and laptops? Inside you had to talk with people, really talk. They also had stationery to write letters and board games to play. It was a true mecca in the ever-changing Nashville and one of the places I always took people when they came to visit me. Unfortunately, the tea shop blew away in the tornado in 2020. Leah and her husband weren't able to rebuild for various reasons. Maybe that's why I miss them even more. But I digress.

It wasn't long after my mother's diagnosis that I went in, down-trodden and sad. I sought out Leah, and we sat and talked as we often did. I need to mention that no matter how many people came to talk to Leah, she never hurried you or looked over your shoulder. If you were talking to her, you were the most important person in the world. I hope I make people feel like Leah makes people feel.

I told her about my mom. I told her that I *needed* to talk to my mom about dying and what would happen after she died. Leah gently stopped me.

"Does your mother believe she is going to beat cancer?"

"Yes, with everything she has."

"Then stop trying to talk to her about dying every time you get on the phone with her." (My mom had recently admonished me for this. She said it made her sad.)

"Ok," I stammered. "But, but, but I need . . ." I trailed off with tears streaming down my face.

She kept going, even more gently now. "If she believes she is going to be healed, then give her the greatest gift and believe with her."

I walked out of High Garden different from the woman who walked in. And from that moment forward until three months before her death, we stopped talking about her dying and we lived. We believed. We danced. We savored the time we had, however long that might be.

My mom and I took one last majestic girls' trip to Maine the fall before she passed. I was speaking to every male athlete at the

University of Maine. She had a front-row seat for my talk. I can still see her and her beautiful face below her bandanna (her hair had recently said "sayonara"). She had a look of both pride and anguish as I shared about being dragged from one end of the house to the other by someone who claimed to love me. She was my greatest fan. And I learned to be hers. What a gift.

After all, I knew what her heart sounded like from the inside. What intimacy, my word. And to think that I could've missed out on this because it was hard and complicated. I beg of you, beloved, don't look away, don't run away when it's hard and complicated. If you don't flee in hard times, the courage that it takes to stay is the breeding ground for relentless joy. That's when we as flawed humans need each other the most. And it's these hard, complicated relationships that have tremendous potential to be so very amazing if we are willing to hold our gaze, to not look away.

In some ways, it might have been easier not to be present when my mother left this planet, but I would've missed the last earth-side gift she gave me. The hospice nurse told us my mother's body was slowly shutting down. Just as God forms and breathes life into a baby, the opposite things happen as the human machine prepares to shut down. The nurse told us that hearing was the last of the senses to go. My mother was not really conscious, eyes closed, rattling more than breathing. I snuggled up next to her and whispered in her ear that it was okay to go, that I would be okay. She had spent her life comforting me; it was my time to comfort her, even if it was a half-truth that I would indeed be okay.

Just then, one magnificent tear rolled down her cheek. She had heard me. She was gone minutes later. I had given her permission to let go and fall into the arms of Jesus. Now, if I had chosen to look away, trying to avoid the pain, I would have missed this seminal moment. I am so profoundly grateful I chose to hold my gaze. You can too, my dear.

DON'T LOOK AWAY. You might miss the epic comeback-story-kind-of-love I had with my mom.

On that last trip we took together, we drove all over Maine, having the grandest adventures. I even booked this cabin on Airbnb that had a rocky crag overlooking a pond. It was epic. I awoke one morning and found her gone from the very primitive cabin. She was on that rocky point in an Adirondack chair singing hymns. I snuck up on her with a camera, trying to be stealthy like a mountain lion. She eventually sensed my presence. A smile adorned her majestic face as she turned to face me. Looking back, we both knew that we *could* be squeezing in a lifetime of mother-daughter trips into this one. We didn't want to admit it, but we were both afraid.

A dear friend told me how one day her husband came home and found her crying, missing her mom (who also passed from cancer). "What's wrong?" he asked innocently enough.

She said she bellowed back at him something to the effect of "It will always be wrong to have to live without my mama. There isn't anything wrong with me *today*. It's every freaking day!"

That about sums it up. I often share this story to tell people not to be afraid to mention someone's lost loved one. Most of us want you to bring them up; that's the way their memory stays alive. We want to tell stories about them and laugh and cry and not feel you tense up with anxiety. Don't be afraid that you'll crack our fragile grieving souls. You won't. I promise.

Dare to wade into the waters of grief with us. And you, the griever, invite others in by not hiding your grief—by openly admitting when you are hurting and speaking about your lost loved ones. There is healing there. Healing together.

Here's the most beautiful part of this story: while no one, and I mean no one, will ever be my mama, or yours (or your dad, your child, your friend, your granddad, your lost sibling), there will be people who will come around you and love you who will be shades of them.

Trust me on this.

I have my aunt Karen, who never had her own children and has become one of my stand-in moms. I have another aunt, my aunt

Edda, who gave me her house key after my mama passed. She gently placed the beautifully adorned key in my palm and lovingly closed my fingers around it as if to say, "You have a home with us." (I also lost my dad in 2014, so being truly wanted is pretty profound for me.) My mom's first husband's second wife (I know, right?), Mama Nish, offered to help pay for my wedding. And that doesn't even cover the gobs of true friends who love me through the thickest of thick and the thinnest of thin. I'm talking lifers, people. All shades of my mama. Never will they be her, but they all offer me pieces of her in the here and now, and that is enough on this side of heaven.

I know I can't keep you from the pain—it is inevitable—but what I can do is throw the rope back for you. I have found solid-ish ground to stand on; I won't let you drown in your grief if I can help it. So here goes, here is your part.

Here's your rope: DON'T LOOK AWAY.

At any moment in my mom's cancer journey, I could've tapped out, stayed away, avoided the feelings or the pending loss, or drowned myself in work, but I couldn't. I had learned a painful lesson just five years before when I had looked away and lost my adoptive father unexpectedly.

David Lee Baribeau adopted me, Rachel Joy Grant, when I was eighteen months old and gave me a new name, a life, and the gift of being wanted something fierce. He had red hair and freckles. On our first meeting at my grandmother's house, I crawled up into his lap, soiled my diaper, and nuzzled into his arms. He said it was love at first sight for him. Having no biological kids of his own, I was his world until the day he passed. He and my mom had long since divorced, and he never remarried. He was a salty old army man, and I was his Rae.

In my twenties, he moved to Alabama after living for years in Michigan. I was only a car ride away, but at that point in my life, I was self-absorbed and selfish, trying to fill holes the size of Texas from what I didn't really know yet were daddies issues. That's right, *daddies*, plural. I like to say my sitcom would've been named, *My*

Three Dads. I had a stepdad, an adoptive father, and a biological dad I met at age eleven. (It did not compute in my little brain that David Lee Baribeau was, in fact, NOT the father of Rachel Joy Baribeau.) I can just see us all on *The Maury Povich Show.*

But in real life, my parents were much more thoughtful than that. Apparently, they told me when I was six, but seeing as the Smurfs were much more interesting, I didn't much care. I went back to my cartoons. I can imagine their relief.

"We didn't traumatize her! Whew!"

Turns out I just saved the trauma for later. Lucky me.

As an adult in my twenties, I didn't see my adoptive father but a handful of times a year, even though I was only hours away. I was simply just too important and so was my social life. What I wouldn't give now for one of those weekends back to ride like the wind to Stanford, Alabama. Heck, what I wouldn't give for a nanosecond in his arms. And because he died suddenly and alone, I had massive amounts of guilt and regret.

I hate regret the most. He's a nasty bedfellow. I don't recommend him in any form or dosage.

I hid this guilt very well until large weeping eczema spots came up on both legs and stubbornly refused to bid their adieu. It lasted for the better part of four months. For a season, people, for a whole season! It was gross, embarrassing, and painful. I remember sitting in a waiting room one day and a stranger looked over at me and spoke some of the sweetest and truest words I've ever heard.

"Why are you holding it in?" she asked.

Huh? Me? Who are you? I thought.

But she saw me. She saw the pain and the guilt I was carrying like an albatross around my neck. I walked out of that office knowing I had encountered an angel that day. She was speaking to and acknowledging the pain, regret, and guilt I had for being an absent daughter, for being selfish and broken, and for my papa dying alone. My body was keeping the score, crying out for me to properly process the emotions I was keeping stuffed inside. (*The*

Body Keeps the Score by Bessel van der Kolk is an actual book, and I highly recommend it.)

From that moment forward, I made an eternal promise to myself: I would do the very best I could to live a life of no regret. I would tell that person at the grocery store that their eyes glitter like the sun bouncing off the sand, I would go for that audacious opportunity, take the job far away, tell that person I love them or I am sorry.

I would take the trip.

No regrets.

And a crazy thing happened along the way. Those large spots weeping constantly on my legs? They stopped weeping and cleared up.

The loss of my daddycakes, as he was called, helped me bear the loss of my mother better in some ways, because my mom and I took the trips, we giggled and cried, we said what we needed to say, we danced and we planned, and we pretended like cancer wasn't the third wheel in the beautiful relationship we had created.

NO REGRETS. NONE.

Real talk here: none of us know our time, and we are all just walking each other home. It's not if; it's when. Let's not waste the time we have.

Real talk here: none of us know our time, and we are all just walking each other home. It's not if; it's when. Let's not waste the time we have.

It's the only way I can look back on losing my mama with some semblance of peace.

For some who are reading this, you're still there, in the thick of IT! Holding back, holding on to your regrets like a toddler and their soiled, nasty blanket they can't bear to let go of.

I feel you. I see you. I am with you because I've been where you are. Let it go, give it up. Regret is not your friend. It's a punisher that wants to keep you bound.

I've found it helpful to turn to the sky and talk to my daddy, to tell him I'm sorry. I think he would be really proud of the woman I've become. And talking to Jesus is always a great answer. He knows all my regrets and my sins (and yours), both public and hidden. When I give it all to HIM, it is nailed to the cross forevermore. I don't have to wrestle with it like the devil wants me to. I am free to live a life of peace, joy, and love. Unencumbered, beautiful, compassionate, and strong—here I am.

I might be a little worse for wear, but I love this me.

All of me. Finally.

And I'm holding the rope, ready to throw it back for you. I want this same freedom, passion, and happiness for you. If you choose not to look away from the difficult stuff, you, too, can make sense and peace with your past—you can learn from the mistakes. Take it from me, I didn't think I would lose another parent at such a young age. But I did, and I was able to draw upon my past mistakes so that I wasn't doomed to repeat them.

But it took making a conscious decision, an "I'm going to be present and not going to miss a moment" kind of energy. An "I'm going to punch regret in the throat" kind of energy. The "you aren't welcome here, buddy" kind of energy.

Is there someplace in your life that needs you to give it another look, another gaze, another glance? Somewhere that pain might be lurking? Or unresolved emotions? Don't look away, because beneath all of that is healing. When we turn our attention to the difficult and painful things in our lives, in time we find healing, and then we find a good and beautiful way forward.

Trust me. Don't look away.

I literally cannot wait to hear what happens in your life when you keep your eyes open!

JOYSTART

I was on a magazine cover that went into eleven hundred prisons. Inside the pages, I gave my testimony. My advice to those readers? Whether you are in a literal prison or a prison of your own mind, you can write a letter to the person you wronged. I'd encourage you to do the same. If that person is no longer living, I would encourage you to still write the letter. It will be cathartic for your soul. And maybe you want to take it one step further and write one to their next of kin. It's a bold step, but bold healing comes from stepping out in faith! And maybe that letter is to you. Maybe you need to forgive yourself.

Also consider journaling about the following questions:

When was a time you saw the shade of a lost loved one in somebody else? How did they encourage you in your grief?

What are some things and people in your life that could benefit from another look, from more of your attention? Where might past regret be stealing from your present?

CHAPTER 5

The Gift of Pain

This chapter is hard to write. It might be hard to read too. But this is what I know—without a doubt: the more we talk about mental health and our own struggles, the less power and shame they hold, the less stigma they carry.

So together let's do a breathing exercise. Why do I want you to do a breathing exercise a few chapters into my book? Because it's a beautiful and useful technique when things feel too heavy or too painful. I also suspect this chapter will be triggering to some. Feel free to come back to this exercise as often as you need throughout this chapter (and throughout your entire life).

So I know this might seem silly, but indulge me. My friend Lindsay Freeman, our resident mindfulness expert at #ImChangingthe Narrative, taught me the 6-2-6 method. Breathe in for six counts, hold for two counts, breathe out for six counts. Repeat up to ten times. I have literally walked anxiety right out of my car with this technique. BUH-BYE! Once I learned this exercise, I started to pay attention to my breathing, and more often than not, it is shallow. I'm willing to bet yours might be too. I hope you commit this to memory for the next time you feel overwhelmed, stressed, worn out, or angry.

In this chapter we will be looking closely at some hard but worthy truths, beginning with this: the things we hide can take us out. In my movement, we call this "wearing a mask." Not a Covid mask but the mask you wear to hide yourself from the world. I know firsthand the damage that can be done by wearing this kind of mask because my mask almost killed me.

I had just lost my mama. I had all the support in the world, but I used my phone and social media to isolate myself. "I'm fine!" I insisted. "Getting better every day." I used the phrase as a mantra to myself and others.

But in reality, I wasn't "getting better." Nor was I dealing with just one loss. My longtime boyfriend and I had also split up right before my mama passed. So my heart was shattered romantically, and I lost my mommy. A broken heart times two. Life can be incredibly cruel sometimes. Typing it still doesn't do the pain justice. It was that horrific. I could never have imagined that kind of pain, but there I was.

And if that wasn't enough, I was practically flat broke. I had spent the last ten months focused on my mom and a smidgen on the movement. I don't regret that for a millisecond though. I helped her with exploratory treatments not covered by insurance, juiced real fruits and veggies daily, and supplied her with bottles and bottles of supplements. These things add up. And when she needed things or to take trips, I paid so she would have the least amount of stress possible. I took care of my mama in a lot of ways, and for that I am proud. But there was little left over afterward. And with no steady pay since I wasn't out on the road speaking much—and the house payments still coming—I was in over my head.

After spending a few weeks grieving in Alabama (in her home) and laying her to rest, I made my way back to Nashville where I lived. I distinctly remember a moment on the drive home, passing through the hills of north Alabama, when I actually told myself,

You're fine. She's in a better place. You got this. You prepared for this. You had ten months.

Friends, let me tell you, that was the grief and shock talking. You can never truly prepare yourself for losing a parent, much less living in a world without them. And really, do you ever get over losing a mother? Or a father? The answer is a resounding no! I know people who had terrible parents but still mourn and miss them. It's just a fact of life. I know people who are mourning parents still living. They are mourning who they should have been, who they could have been. I know people who lost their parents when they were young, barely old enough to remember, and they miss their parents dearly. I will miss my parents until the day I take my last breath, but then I believe they, along with God, will meet me at the pearly gates.

Once I made it home to Nashville, the aching depression and anxiety set in (along with the double heartbreak). It was the July after she passed, and I was getting up super-duper early for Sirius shows. The second night, I found myself tossing and turning, constantly looking at the clock and counting the hours I would get if I could just fall asleep at that instant. Hello insomnia, my old friend. I hope to never see you again. It was the kind of insomnia where every problem that has *ever* plagued you or could possibly plague you fifteen years down the road torments you. Yep, overthinking on steroids. I tossed and turned in hopes of finding a better sleeping position, but it was hopeless. When 3:00 a.m. rolled around, I knew I was screwed.

I am going to suck on the air this morning. I am going to lose my job because of it, I told myself.

What happened next still shakes me to my core. I heard a literal voice in my ear say, "You're going to lose everything. You are worthless. A loser. You can't keep anything. See, your parents are gone, and so is your boyfriend. You're going to lose your house. No one will ever book you again. You're a failure."

I've heard people say they've heard voices, beloved, but mine was a singular voice, and it sounded like what I imagine a snake would sound like if it spoke. Just typing these words makes me shudder all over again. Imagine for a moment a snakelike, slithering voice whispering in your ear. I'm quite sorry you have to read these words right now, but my hope is to connect with someone or multiple someones who have heard the same things I have.

I'm going to say this often: You are not alone. You are not defective. You are not broken. You are loved. You are valuable, and your life matters greatly!

I tried to silence the voice but to no avail. It wouldn't stop. And when the voice wouldn't stop, a new thought entered my mind. I saw myself walking down the carpeted stairs, getting my father's revolver off the top of my refrigerator, putting it in my mouth, and ending it all. I cried out to God in all of this. I bawled and cried out for help in my bedroom.

I'm going to say this often: You are not alone. You are not defective. You are not broken. You are loved. You are valuable, and your life matters greatly!

That same dark voice told me, "You can't call anyone. You will burden them at this time of night." So I didn't reach out to anyone. What a shame that I didn't think I could call anyone.

Friend, listen to me. This may be one of the most important things you ever hear me say: people would rather share your burdens than carry your casket. That is powerful! This one truth could have helped me that night. I almost took myself out of this world because I believed a lie. My gracious, I have no idea how long this "battle" lasted, but I do know at some point I fell asleep from sheer exhaustion.

I woke an hour or so later for that SiriusXM show feeling like I had run three emotional and physical marathons. I was snotty and tender. I remember my producer asking if I was all right. I lied and said it was just allergies.

After that day, I wrestled with whether to talk about this. The same voice from that night said, "You can't talk about this. You'll never get booked to speak again. They will know you are broken, defective, and weak."

But even as this evil voice hissed lies into my ear, there was another voice. (Oh boy, was there another voice!) A good voice. A loving voice. It was the voice of our Papa God. And He said (I feel like there needs to be a horn accompaniment here and a gospel choir singing this part), "My girl, you are a warrior! You tell them! Tell them far and wide, tell them they aren't defective, they aren't broken! Tell them they aren't alone!"

So I did. So I do. And I will continue until I take my last breath.

Not even a week later, I sat in my makeshift studio in East Nashville and made a video that would change the trajectory of my life and many others.[1] I told the story of the night I almost took my own life. I was raw. I was honest. I was broken but I was free.

I took my mask off. I was no longer bound by shame. I found freedom in radical vulnerability, in showing up battered and bruised but mighty like a warrior. My story had light piercing through it, and there was magnificent beauty in my brokenness. Not long after, a very prominent gymnast, Olivia Gunter—whom I fell in love with during my days speaking on her college campus—saw the video and told me she was so inspired by my radical vulnerability that she made her own video about eating disorders and body dysmorphia in the sport of collegiate gymnastics and beyond. As I watched the numbers skyrocket on her video in a short period of time, I knew that I was running my predetermined race. I was exactly where I needed to be. I think Genesis 50:20 is pertinent here: "You intended to harm me, but God intended it for good to accomplish what is now being done, the saving of many lives."

I truly believe the devil was that serpentlike voice in my ear. I also believe there was a great battle waged in my room that night. The devil meant to take me out. I have zero doubt about that. He hates me and he hates you. He hates our marriages and our children; he hates light and life and joy. And every time I or you lean into our

God-given joy, I know it makes him bellow in the halls of hell. Take that, you creature!

Light wins in the end! Love wins in the end!

We all have our own experiences when it comes to mental health struggles (whether it's you or someone you love).

Get my drift?

Loving Jesus doesn't mean you won't face mental health struggles. No ma'am, no sir, it does not make you exempt.

If I had a magical megaphone that the whole world could hear (and maybe this book is just that), I would say this: you need Jesus. But you also might need therapy or medication to manage your mental health. I think we would lose a lot fewer people if that message was widely known. I also think God has mightily equipped some amazing souls called therapists, counselors, psychologists, and psychotherapists to do their jobs. I think they are running their race through their chosen profession. And they were called for a reason.

There is also this: in the dark, pain is amplified and problems become bigger when you can't see them clearly for what they are. Isolation is the breeding ground for shame to grow, pain to be magnified, and problems to become hairier. I should know. That's how I got into trouble so quickly.

People ask me a lot about my journey after my Dark Night of the Soul and what my healing pilgrimage has looked like. I became ultracognizant of the fine line between solitude and isolation. I rather like being alone, but in a jiffy, sweet solitude can turn into isolation if we aren't careful. I stopped using text messages to feign being in a positive place. I started answering calls and letting people pour out all of their love and concern for me. I couldn't afford therapy, so I went to my pastor, JD Ost, and told him my situation. My church lined me up with a professional who was able to see me soon after. I went to my banker to face my financial pain. I made a dentist appointment, a lady doctor appointment, and an appointment for a mammogram.

And I went home to my mother's house to face the pain of being there without her. I thought it would be too painful to go to her house, to *our* home, to where she passed, but when I was finally brave enough to do it, the most spectacular and surprising thing happened. I found her everywhere. In the walls, in her knickknacks and dishes, in the air, on her back porch swing, in her kitchen. It wasn't painful, like I expected. Instead, she enveloped me—her spirit, her life force, her memories, the mark she left in her home, all of it. I felt her in my bones and all around me. I still do when I make my way back to Pell City, Alabama.

Here's what else I know: the devil meant to take me out, but he actually gave me the blueprint to be able to save millions of lives. And even more amazing and serendipitous was the fact that the first online course I was to teach (aptly named The Blueprint) was supposed to be a recorded course with no live interaction. At the very last minute, I heard the Lord say, "Do it live. Give them all you've got." Because of that seemingly simple yet profoundly seminal decision, two people had the chance to meet online in the intimate confines of my course and subsequently fall in love. My, oh my!

HIYAH! Take that, Satan! His plans included taking me out, silencing me, and breaking a lot of hearts in the process, but instead, he gave me a story, a scar, and the ability to say to someone else, "I've been there. I know how you're feeling. You are not alone."

And that is exactly what I did. That same summer I went to speak to the University of Minnesota football program and gave my first full talk on mental health. I bared my soul, everything that I just shared with you. I then held up the microphone and courageously called out, "Who wants to take their mask off too?" My heart was thudding out of my chest. A cold sweat came across my brow. If no one took this mic, I was going to look like a fool. There was no coming back from this if no one stood to share; there was no graceful way to land this plane. I was out there flying, gloriously I might add, with no backup plan.

The seconds ticked by like minutes. I saw players nervously shift and look around. I was near the point of giving up, licking my wounds, and going home, just standing there with a mic raised passionately above my head, when someone said, "I'll go."

Dear sweet baby Jesus, thank you! I uttered in my spirit.

After he shared, another shared, and another, and another. I won't divulge in detail what they discussed, but they did it in front of one another. It was intimate stuff pertaining to family issues, addictions, homesickness, and depression. They yelled out in support of one another, they hugged, they fist-bumped, they high-fived. Many of them saw each other, truly, for the first time. It was radical. Like nothing else I've ever been a part of. And it was born from my own pain.

Let me say that again!

It was a truly miraculous gift born of my own pain.

There are gifts waiting on you, too, when you take your mask off and get real with yourself and others.

The meeting went way over time-wise, but Coach P.J. Fleck knew how important it was. There are others out there who would've been prisoners to their schedules. Schedules are great and all, but sometimes, in the face of such radical healing, you have to be willing to flex. Thank you for flexing, P.J.! He (along with his precious wife and rock, Heather) is one of the most vocal and dedicated college football coaches when it comes to promoting mental health in his program and beyond. It's an everyday thing for him and his staff. I am so blessed to be called family in that program.

I stick around after my talks. I stay till the last player or coach wants to talk. I give out my number and my contact info. I know it's radical to be that available, but it is what I feel led to do. That day, and at many talks after, I had many players, law enforcement, and everyday people coming up to me and sharing that they had heard a voice/voices too. They had taken the pills, they had cut themselves. I even had a player tell me he almost drove off the road intentionally on the way to hear me speak because he felt so hopeless. When he heard my story, he knew he was meant to be alive.

And I will never forget the night the world stopped revolving just a bit when I held a woman in my arms, who said through sobs, "I was going to kill myself tonight, and then I heard you. I had already written the letter. Now I'm going to call my family and tell them that

I'm struggling and am going to get help." I held on to her just as tight as she did me, our tears commingling on our cheeks, streaming down both our faces. My story had altered the course of this woman's life. It was literally a life-or-death moment. I remember sitting in my car long after I had shared my testimony that night, bawling like a baby.

This was the gift of my pain.

Listen to me carefully. Your pain is not only for you. If you are bold enough to be able to talk about it, to share it, there is someone on your path that needs to hear it. They need to hear that what was meant to kill you, didn't. And, in fact, you are here to tell your story boldly!

I am often asked, "What if my story isn't traumatic? I've had a pretty good, uneventful life."

Listen to me, your pain doesn't have to be traumatic. It can be anything you have overcome! Anything!

And with our pain, we have two choices—to become bitter or better.

The choice, my love, is up to you.

But I can tell you, without a doubt, that joy is found in choosing the better. It's not too late to give up the bitterness, to lay it down, to forgive that person, especially if it's you. And I want to pause here and tell you that just because you forgive someone doesn't mean they deserve a front-row seat in your life's auditorium. They might not get admission anymore, but it does mean you've released them, the pain, the bitterness, and the weight of unforgiveness. Others may work their way back inside. They will earn it, step-by-step. And good on them if they do. Others are best loved from a distance. Trust me on this.

No, it's not too late. As long as you are breathing, there is a chance to change your narrative and chase joy with a fervor that will make hell nervous.

I also want to give you a battle plan if you or anyone you care about gets into trouble mentally. And I have to credit my business manager and dear friend, Jason Parker, for this nugget: if you get to where I was that night, you need to have three people you can call, text, or reach out to. I like to call these three people your *ride or die*. They are the ones you would call if you just won the lottery or if you only had ramen noodles in the pantry; they would come change a tire for you or lend moral support while someone else is doing it. Quite simply, they love you when you have a lot and love you just the same when you have little.

I often have people ask me, "Should I tell them they are my ride or die?"

Yes, TELL THEM! And then tell them to go find their three people so that it spreads like a ripple on a pond.

If you call one and can't get them, call the next, and then the next. The fourth call is to the Suicide and Crisis hotline: 1-800-273-8255. (Add that number to your contacts.) If you're in a really bad place, then call your first ride or die and then immediately call the crisis hotline. Or call the crisis hotline and text your people at the same time, but by all means, do not suffer alone.

That night, if I'd had this plan, I would not have had to go through that pain and fear in isolation. The lie I believed that night was that my people would be burdened by my pain.

What a crock of crap!

My people told me, "I would have been torn to shreds if you went through with it. I'm hurt you didn't let me know you were that troubled and felt like you couldn't call." They forgave me because I explained what I went through. I explained the depression and anxiety I was experiencing and that the devil deceived me.

I have one last nugget of joy in this chapter before we continue in our journey. (PS I love you, and I'm so grateful you chose to pick up this book or download it to listen to!)

Are you ready? What if I told you I had a powerful phrase that I say to my problems now.

Here it is. Ready?

"SO WHAT?"

So what if I fail? So what if I lose my house? So what if I'm broken?

In my mind, I go back and say, "So what?" to so many things from that night. So what if you go broke? So do millions of others and they bounce back. So what if you lose your house? You will find another and rebuild. So what if your marriage is falling apart? Get your shovel and do the work necessary to repair it, and if it still isn't going to work, then you know you fought like the dickens to save it. So what if you get your heart broken? Better to be broken than to never truly live, or love. So what if you lose your job? There are more amazing jobs out there, or maybe it's time to start that business you've always dreamed of starting.

It's time to get your joy back, baby!

It's time to choose better!

It's time to enact a battle plan and share it with all your people and memorize it in your collective hearts for times of crisis.

I love you.

I see you.

I am so darn proud of you.

JOYSTART

Here are some questions to ask yourself. Write your answers in the journaling section:

What have I been through that could possibly help others?

What gift could come from my pain?

Am I currently choosing to become bitter or better?

Who are my three ride or dies? What's stopping me from telling them now and buying them this book? (You knew I was going to add that, right? I want this book's message to spread far and wide!)

CHAPTER 6

The Garden Tomb

It was May 2018, and I was sitting in a corner of a bus full of strangers trying to make myself small because I was silently sobbing. A dream I'd had for so long had received the final nail in the coffin. I had been turned down for the final time on a book proposal I had worked on for four-plus months. And let me fill you in on a secret: writing a book proposal is painstaking, laborious, detailed, and thorough, and many of those traits do not come naturally to me. I am creative, free, a little messy, wonderfully clumsy in body and spirit, and fully magical. (You better know yourself!)

So here I am on this bus with a group of people I've barely met as we're preparing to depart for Israel, and I'm asking God, *Why? Why would you do this to me just before I leave on this trip of my dreams, this trip to the Holy Land?*

I heard him reply in my spirit, *I want all of you these next few days.*

I heard it like you hear a hungry baby cry in the dead of night. God didn't want half of my attention; He wanted *all of it.*

And later I would learn why.

What if our most crushing circumstance is really just preparation? God crushed my dreams of authorship (at that moment in my life) to get my attention. We look at crushing circumstances with our human mind. I know I do. They are painful, a letdown, and heartbreaking, but what if we were bold enough to start looking for clues in our crushing circumstances?

When we feel disappointed the most, what if we were heaven-minded enough to ask, What is coming, what is this for, what are You preparing me for?

I'm not a covert crier, by the way. I have never been good at hiding my emotions. And for many years of my life, I spent my days trying to shrink down—shrink down my larger-than-life emotions, shrink down my charisma, my loudness, my personality, all of it. So here I was on a bus to the airport, trying to hide this soul-crushing news as I set off for a trip I had dreamed of for so many years.

When we feel disappointed the most, what if we were heaven-minded enough to ask, What is coming, what is this for, what are You preparing me for?

And making this dream trip even more sacred to me was the fact that my mother had done extensive genealogy research in the years before I left. She discovered that we were Sephardic Jews.

Studying my recent and ancient ancestry, I am—among other things—Mayan, Italian, Chinese (very far back), Mexican, Colombian, Peruvian, Spanish, Jewish, and English. If ever there were a Heinz 57 person—in other words a person of many origins—I am her and she is me.

And I love her . . . ahem . . . me.

Anyway, back to my story.

After arriving in Israel, there were so many aha moments, so many "OHHH MAY GAHHH, THIS IS THE BIBLE IN REAL LIFE" moments. I saw mosaics from Jesus's time. I got baptized, again, in the Sea of Galilee. I rode a boat across the Sea of Galilee that resembled what boats looked like when Jesus walked this earth.

And somewhere out on the water, our group broke out in spontane-
ous worship. I sailed that sea with hands raised, croaking out a tune
with tears streaming down my face.

When the boat ride ended and we reached the other side, we had
dinner at a charming restaurant perched out on a long pier. Just so
you can imagine it, the Sea of Galilee is more like a medium-sized
lake. Our tour guide's grandfather joined us at that dinner. He was
the cutest old man. I simultaneously wanted to squeeze him and
also be very quiet and soak up his wisdom. I have a thing for history and kids and old people. And this little old man stole my heart.

I complimented him and that's all it took. He began to tell me
his story. His grandson Yoav, our tour guide, translated for him. We
hung on his grandfather's every word as I furiously scribbled notes
in my journal to try and preserve this moment in time.

Yochanan Viner was born in Poland in what he estimates was
1928. Where he was born is now a part of Ukraine. When he was
around twelve, Hitler had already ordered the invasion of Poland,
and WWII was underway. According to him, Germany hinted to
the Ukrainians and other people groups with a history of hostility
toward Jews as to the terror the Jews were about to face. To those
who already hated or despised Jews, this was taken as permission
to treat Jewish people poorly. Yochanan and his family were forced
into a Jewish ghetto along with every other Jew in the city.

> I had a very smart mother, and she saw what was coming. Father
> could not see the future, he was more reserved. I survived because
> of my mother. In the nighttime, my mother woke me up, hugged me,
> and opened the door to [the gate surrounding] the ghetto. I asked
> how she knew when to open the door, because there were Ukrainian
> soldiers on guard. For weeks she would stay up and not sleep, and
> she would monitor the guards' schedule to see when they would go
> urinate. And then she would know when there is a chance to take
> me out. . . . My mother grabbed me in her arms, opened the door
> of the ghetto with her leg and pushed me into the snow. Outside it
> was snowing, and I fell from the step of the apartment and was in

snow up to my hips; and each step I had to use my hands to get my feet out of the snow and that's how I moved forward. My mother said, "go, my son" and that ended my conversation and rendezvous with my mother. I never saw my mother and father and younger brother again.[1]

Pause for a second and put yourself in his mother's shoes. It's hard to fathom this kind of sacrificial love. She knew the only hope for her son to live was to get him out of the ghetto. Not take him with her and her husband, but to literally push her child out into the snow, totally alone, to save his life with no regard for her own. My gracious. This level of devotion, this yielding of her own flesh and blood, is almost beyond comprehension. (Gratitude break: God did this same thing for us when He sacrificed His Son on the cross.) Yet it happened over and over again during the Holocaust, families separating and sacrificing familial bonds to try and ensure a life beyond the war.

I was shook.

Yochanan went to live in the woods for almost two years, most of that time alone until he was joined by an old schoolmate whose family had just been murdered in front of his eyes. He was shot through the neck. Yochanan used his own urine to clean and nurse his friend's wound. They would go out at night, under the cover of darkness, and scavenge for food. People would covertly give them bread with pig fat stuffed inside. That is how they survived. Two young boys, living in the woods, alone: ratty, greasy, unkempt, dirty, and dressed in rags, but each with a heart of a lion and the will to live. And here I was sitting across from this living legend, this hero, this walking, talking, breathing piece of our past.

When you are in the middle of a beautiful moment, space, or time, do you ever think, *How in the world am I sitting in this place, seeing/hearing this, experiencing these feelings and emotions. Am I really having this experience? Really, God? Me?*

But in a good way like, *Wow, God, You would let me experience this? I feel so unworthy of this grandeur.*

That's how I felt sitting at that table. I could literally reach out and touch a warrior who had lived in the woods, mostly alone, for two years after his mother courageously saved his life. In these moments, I will pinch my own arm and mimic taking a picture with my own two hands to cement the memory in my mind.

Beyond his mother's courage, there was also the gumption of another woman who surely saved his life. According to his grandson Yoav:

> In the beginning, while hiding in the forest, he would go to a barn near the forest where some Czech people were living. His mom told him to go there; she used to work with them and make heavy winter jackets for them. The Czechs let him stay in the barn and eat the animals' food. But after a while they told him that he could not stay anymore, so he went back to the forest and hid. He used to go once in a while to the houses of these Czech families.
>
> According to what he shares, there was one time he got confused and knocked on the wrong door; a woman answered with her robe open, hastily covering her lady parts with her robe. Inside was a Ukrainian officer cleaning his pistol. My grandfather was very filthy and dirty and had long hair. The Ukrainian policeman was showing off for the woman and yelled, "You want to see how I kill the filthy Jew?" He was about to shoot my grandfather. Then she opened the robe and told him if you're going to kill him, you won't see these again and you won't get this anymore! My grandfather ran for his life. So she basically saved him from this policeman who was about to kill him.

I wanted to hug Yochanan, this living legend sitting across from me. What a present he was, in human form, and to think if I hadn't engaged or inspected this gift of a person, I might've missed him altogether. Good gracious, good gracious indeed!

And remember how we talked about acknowledging beautiful moments? You don't have to be sitting across from a Holocaust survivor; it could be the giggle of your child, ringing the bell after beating cancer, or teaching your child how to drive and living to tell about it. Friend, there is such joy in the acknowledging and the savoring of the "oh my gosh, this is happening" moments. Commit them to memory and heart so you can forever be grateful.

And let me drop a truth bomb on you: I'd much rather be the person who thinks too many things are miracles rather than the other way around. Because if I were more cynical than joyful, that would mean I would miss them—the little explosions of joy and knowing that are sent for us daily. Often, we are just too busy or broken to notice them, and I have to think that breaks God's heart.

I'm not saying you are wrong in nature if you were born cynical and find it to be one of your better traits, but this is an appeal to invite joy to the party as well. You can be cynical and joyful. What a beautiful balance that could be!

There are so many moments throughout this book when I invite you to put yourself in my shoes or the shoes of others. I think back to that night, sitting on the banks of that magnificent sea. If I had given in to my disappointment over not getting a book deal—wallowing in my dismay and shriveling away from life, people, and all that is good and holy—I would've missed this sacred encounter.

There are times, like this one, when I shined in the face of disappointment, but there are also times when I certainly shriveled. We are human beings; we make mistakes. We shrivel like fruit, but sometimes we surprise even ourselves and sweeten in the face of disaster. This moment is to pause and ponder, maybe take note of your past responses (the good and the bad) in the face of disappointment. Write them down if you feel so led. And next time you feel the sting of disappointment, I want you to whisper to yourself, "I will not shrivel like rotten fruit. I'm going to sweeten in this situation like a big, ripe, juicy grapefruit!" (Sidenote: it's hard not to smile when you think of yourself as a grapefruit in all your dang glory!)

Toward the end of our trip to Israel, we visited the Garden of the Tomb where Jesus is thought to have been buried. Nothing could prepare me for what I found beyond those historic walls. Have you ever stopped to ponder heaven? What it might truly be like? Losing as many people as I have will make you think of heaven often.

Well, let me tell you, I think I stood about as close to heaven as I could in the earthly realm when I entered the Garden of the Tomb. Inside there were many groups touring, but oddly it never felt crowded. And there were people represented from every corner of this beautiful, amazing world. There were Asians and Africans and Nordic people, to name just a few.

After we saw Golgotha—the hill Jesus was crucified on—we circled back to a smallish area for our group to have some worship time and take communion. As we were singing, I turned and heard another group coming from above us, singing their little hearts out too. It was a heavily accented—to me at least—hymn from my childhood. It was a surreal and beautiful moment.

That's what my version of heaven looks like, folks: pink, purple, black, and white, we are all precious in His sight. I think we'll all be speaking our own languages, but we will be fluent in the greatest of these, the heart language. We will just *get* each other and love each other deeply, in an instant. That's Rachel Joy's abridged version of heaven, at least. The Bible tells us:

> After this I looked, and there before me was a great multitude that no one could count, from every nation, tribe, people and language, standing before the throne and before the Lamb. They were wearing white robes and were holding palm branches in their hands. (Rev. 7:9)

As our praise and worship time was coming to an end, it was time for our group to visit the tomb where many historians believe Jesus's body was actually laid. Three-fourths of our group took communion and left our little private area to head to there, but for some reason, I and two others stayed behind. The only way I know to describe it is being slain in the Spirit. I still have the tissues I used to hopelessly dab my face as the tears gushed. It was just a moment, but one I will never forget. I felt as if Jesus was holding me tight in a bear hug.

We eventually made our way over to the tomb. Just before I stooped to go in, a lively group of beautiful Asian women enveloped me in a circle. They gave me a "love" keychain that I still treasure to this day. I turned back to the tomb and went in. It was just me and my two traveling companions inside. I stood against the wall, red-faced and bawling like a child. The gravity of the location hit me, and it left a mark. He had lain there, right there, after paying the ultimate sacrifice.

And He rose from there too.

The enormity of it all is a heavy burden to really ponder. I can't say for sure how long we spent in that tomb, but what happened next solidified everything I know to be true about God. As I stooped again to leave, I clearly heard God whisper to me, "My girl, whatever you think is the worst thing that can happen to you, know that I am with you. I will never forsake you nor leave you."

And in my peon brain, the only thing I could make of it at the time was losing my job or my house. That was my worst nightmare, losing worldly things. (Oh, Rachel, you really had your priorities so wrong.) Not to be too hard on myself, I'm not a materialistic person. Maybe I just didn't want to bring myself to think about losing another person. I had already experienced so much loss, my brain just automatically protected me from thinking of more death, more loss.

Looking back, I see why God shut the door on that book deal; He desperately needed my attention. He was getting ready to do soul surgery on me. I walked out of that tomb and scurried to the gift shop, not thinking too much about the message that was just laid on my heart. I mean, I heard Him for sure, but the enormity of the message hadn't sunk in yet.

We, the trio, were behind the rest of the group, and I wanted to buy some trinkets. (Anyone else a trinket king/queen like me? I gotta bring back *something*. Coffee mugs and ornaments are my faves.) I rushed up the ramp, giddy with the excitement that only impending shopping can bring. I was about to tear up that gift shop; I needed to remember this magical time in the garden with tangible items from my day there. Plus, I had many gifts to bring home.

I was rushing up the ramp, almost to the Holy Grail of gift shops, when on my right I saw a woman rocking back and forth with her eyes closed, weeping. She was having herself a moment with God, right there out in the open. It looked as if she was just struck by the Spirit right where she was standing, at the entrance to the gift shop, and she gave in to it.

Yay her!

I have to admit, I passed her by. But as I was just about to pull the handle of the door to the gift shop, I again heard the Lord. "Go back. Be with her," He said.

At this point, Jesus and I were on a roll. He was talking, and I was certainly listening. I knew to go back, so I did. I've mentioned the Southern saying once before: I don't know him/her from Adam's house cat. It wholly applied in this instance. I mean, this woman was having a moment, a whole moment, heck maybe it was a full hour she was having. But in any event, here I was being called to lay hands on and pray over a total stranger.

If you're not familiar with the term *lay hands on*, it means to literally lay hands on someone and pray for them. In the nano-seconds that passed as I was circling back to her, I thought that this could go well or I could be sporting a shiner for the rest of my trip in the Holy Land. It really was a 50/50 proposition. But still, I was obedient.

I want you to take a moment to think about this in your own life. Can you say, "But still, I was obedient"? Because I believe there is magic in that, in *the not knowing but the going*. Here am I, Lord. Shiner or no shiner, I'm here to do Your bidding.

I came up next to her and put my hands on her back. I rocked with her. I wept. We prayed. I never got her name, but I'll never forget her face. Afterward, I turned to go back to the gift shop and catch up with my group.

One of the other people in the group who happened to catch this sacred encounter stopped me to say, "I'm really sorry. I thought you were just a sportscaster, but it turns out you are so much more!" Woo-wee, cheers to being seen, not seen with the naked eye, not seen for any physical attribute, but seen for your soul, seen when you reflect Jesus. That is the best kind of beautiful right there.

I hope that lady saw Jesus in me that day. I believe she did.

I flew home from Israel bursting with passion and even more purpose. I had walked with Jesus. I had talked with Jesus. In fact, I had heard from Jesus multiple times. I wanted to share that with everyone who would listen.

I didn't think too much more about that personal message God had whispered to me when leaving the tomb. That is, until almost two months to the day when I was standing in an exam room holding my mama's hand. The doctor said the cancer was stage four.

The air went out of the room as quickly as a bullet leaves a chamber. And honestly, I felt like I had been shot in the chest, in the heart, as I watched my mama struggle to be brave in front of me and my stepdad. At that moment, something in my soul clicked, and the tomb message I had experienced came full circle. He wasn't trying to tell me about losing an earthly possession. Our loving and gracious Papa God was telling me I was going to lose my mommy. He loved me so much He was trying to cushion me; He was trying to comfort me beforehand. I think we all experience personal, radical miracles in our lives if we are open to these sorts of things. This was one of the most radical of my life. I finally realized why they call Him the GOOD Lord. He cradled me as I bled out emotionally from hearing the words "stage four."

She was gone ten months later.

If you've ever been church-hurt or people-hurt and you're mad at God, I would love to reintroduce you to this God, a God who loved me (and you) so much that He wanted to wrap me in Bubble Wrap for the eventual collision.

What a LOVING God.

So many of us walking this planet have the idea that God is legalistic, rigid, and harsh. I don't know Him that way at all, and my tomb experience solidifies that belief. If I get to do anything in this life, I hope to reflect and share the Papa, Abba Father, the God I know.

Maybe you picked up this book and have a complicated relationship with the God of the universe. My hope is that by the end of this book, you think of Him as a pretty rad dude. Yes, I just called Jesus (the Son of God) a rad dude. By all accounts He was. He hung with sinners of all varieties: ladies of the night, thieves, murderers. He told them they were more than their pasts, more than their wrongdoings. That there was hope and a different way to live. If you've been hurt by circumstances or people or the church, could you, would you dare to talk to the Big Man about that? I bet He would have something to share with you.

And for those of you who might be asking yourself right now, "But why didn't He just save your mommy?"

I can't answer that.

But I can tell you a story of my former preacher and his son, Joshua. His son was rushed to the hospital with debilitating headaches when he was around thirteen. After performing some tests, they found a tumor on his brain stem. My pastor was outside, crying out to God, and he shared that he heard God say, "I'm going to take your son. But so many will come to know Me through his story."

The human part of my pastor cried out, "NOO! Not my son," but the part that knew the Lord intimately and how good a God he served knew it was for a purpose. He achingly told us this story from the church stage one Sunday morning. There wasn't a dry eye in the room. So many came to know Christ through the story of Joshua's battle. One of them being me. I rededicated my life not long after doing a story on Joshua and his cancer battle. I was part of the greater plan.

You see, Joshua's story was the catalyst for me to come back to Jesus after my battle with addiction. My mom had been going to the church his father pastored. And she had been asking me to join her because of the relentless love she had for me. She knew if she could get me there to church, Jesus would work on my heart. I just know it is all interconnected. We are all interconnected. Our stories. Our lives. Our pain. Our joy. I don't know why my mommy didn't get her healing this side of heaven or why Joshua didn't either; what I do know is that God made beauty from these ashes.

My gracious, even typing this now makes me weep.

I've gotten countless messages from people who said they took steps to heal their own maternal relationships and wounds after watching my mommy and I battle together for ten months. They said we were inspiring.

I have to agree.

We were, and we are, because that inspiration lives on. I am a living reflection of her.

I carry her with me in my mannerisms, the way I love, forgive, and mother. I am wholly and beautifully Georgia's daughter. And I hope all of those parts of her live on in me. Take the trip. Do the dance. Say what you mean. Clear the slate. Forgive them. Forgive yourself.

I will never be able to quantify the impact of my mother's life. But I am at peace with the good Lord giving her ultimate healing in heaven.

JOYSTART

Is there a time in your life when a crushing event later had an avalanche of impact? Can you look back and see a time when God cradled you before a fall?

In the margins or in the journal section, make a list of who you know God to be. What are His characteristics? Not the person who hurt you, because that grieved God too, to see you hurt, but who do you know God to be? What false images of God have been shown throughout your life?

How might God want to reshape those images for you with His love and kindness?

My list of God's attributes would look something like this:

- Caring
- Comforting
- Ever present
- Faithful
- True to His Word
- Loving
- Powerful

What would your list look like?

CHAPTER 7

The Prodigal Daughter

I t was February 14, 2021, and instead of luxuriating in romance with my fiancé amid roses and chocolate, I was driving in a blinding rainstorm with tears streaming down my face seven hours north. North of pain, north of toxic, north of a failed love and a life that was never meant to be. That's where my soul's GPS wanted to go, anyhow. When I left in my very-used and very-loved 2007 Tahoe loaded with my earthly treasures, I thought I might never see that street again.

Have you ever been in something toxic and reached your breaking point? That's where I was. There was no other way but north, no other way but out.

I reached my lifelong best friend's basement late that night and was immediately greeted by her loving arms and lack of judgment for anyone, lest me. I didn't need to dissect; I just needed to heal. And there in her basement apartment, that's exactly what I did. Me and my little rescue dog, Buddy Jo, took up residence in that basement. And let me tell you, we serve a God who doesn't spare any expense. I loved the couch, I loved the bed, I loved the bathtub, I loved what she made for dinner each week. (And she is big on sitting down for a meal . . . I love it!)

I really loved it all. It was as if all those inanimate objects knew we were coming and were made for a time such as this. And the location wasn't a coincidence either. Jean lives in Pell City where I went to junior high and graduated from high school. My stepdad still lives there in the house he built with my mama, but I couldn't go there. By this time, he already had his own routine, his own life, his own patterns. This is a man I consider a father figure, a man who taught me the art of football by slowly rewinding VHS tapes of games, over and over again, to lovingly teach me the game. He wanted me to come home to his house, my momma's house, but I knew I just needed to hide out. I desperately needed to heal.

I had recently been given the opportunity to work with a fantastic literary agent, which would lead to this very book. There in that basement, a book was born—born from the dark, born from the pain, born from the solitude.

Let me give you a little nugget of wisdom before moving on, a Rachel-ism on solitude: there is a very fine line between isolation and solitude. As someone who quite enjoys my own company, I have to be mindful of when solitude crosses over into isolation. I would caution you to be mindful of that too. It is very easy to cross the line and get into trouble.

> *Let me give you a little nugget of wisdom before moving on, a Rachel-ism on solitude: there is a very fine line between isolation and solitude.*

Very few people knew I was living in my best friend's basement. I preferred it that way, honestly. It afforded me the luxury of nursing my broken heart in privacy. My heart was very much in tatters. My fiancé and I hadn't spoken since I left the home I shared with him on Valentine's Day. There was too much hurt, too much pain and anger lingering between us. All that was left unsaid had a nasty, foul feel to it, so it was probably better if it had time to air out to dry.

So I wrote my book and worked on my movement; I prayed and cried and went upstairs for dinner when it was time. I did this on repeat while wondering whether I should wear my ring. I do a lot in front of the camera, but how could I share my status with others when I didn't even know myself? Leaving it on felt like a betrayal to my best self, and taking it off felt like the final goodbye to the one I thought was my soulmate.

But before I go on, I think it's important for you to know how I got to my best friend's basement. The brokenness in my relationship started before my fiancé and I moved in with one another. After my mom died, I lost my way. Not only was there intimacy outside of marriage, I thought I had to make things happen, speed them up, etc.

To put it simply, I lost my way.

Have you ever lost your way? Hopelessly? Far away from your morals, your standards, far away from yourself? You are not alone; your wandering or lostness has not made you defective or broken or worthless.

Beloved, listen to me, your wandering can make you strong again. It's an invitation to begin again, to crawl back to the path of righteousness, to all you know.

I know this to be true because I lost my mommy on May 1, 2019. On May 30, 2020 (my birthday), I got engaged in the most thoughtful and kind ceremony with my bonus kids and future hubby. Fast-forward to the end of 2020, and I was packing up the first home I had ever purchased in Nashville to move in with my fiancé in Florida, a house he had lovingly purchased for us for our future.

Now, this is where I might lose you, the part where you might argue with me and put down my book, but it's a risk I'm willing to take. Hear me out, please. We've gotten this far together.

I was never supposed to move to Florida. Not yet, at least.

The world will say, "What's the issue?" But biblically speaking, we were playing house. We weren't married yet. He and I had spent the last several years honoring God, ourselves, and each other by saving our physical intimacy for marriage. But after I lost my mama, I lost my way. I lost my north star, my compass, my foundation, and in doing so I lost myself. So I assured myself we were okay. We were going to be married, after all. What could it hurt? God knew he was supposed to be my husband, right? So I rationalized our decision. But the truth is we had missed the mark with our decision—missed what God really wanted for us. I laugh about it now, trying to rationalize my sin with the God of the universe, the God of yesterday and tomorrow and eternity. The God who created literally everything from nothing. As if we could bargain with Him.

All was well in my new home for a while, then the fissures started to appear. It was no one's fault in particular, no blame to lay, other than it just wasn't supposed to be this way. I wasn't supposed to be running desperately out in front of God, trying to flag Him in the direction I thought He should take us. Turns out I am not the best crossing guard in the world, let alone in my life. So it spiraled out of control, so much so that I left in the rain on Valentine's Day.

And that is how I ended up in my best friend's basement—by trying to be the grand crossing guard, the pace car of my own life. As a believer, I know that doesn't work. I only have to sit and ponder my past to know it has never worked. When I have done it my way, apart from God, I have mucked it up. With Him as the pace car, the crossing guard, man, He and I have really gone places.

But I digress. I'm in my best friend's basement, and I'm writing like my life depends on it. Every social engagement I was lovingly invited to I turned down. The only time I came up for air was to eat. And not long after that, I began to travel and speak again. This is what I am born to do, so naturally, it put a pep in my step. I was pumped. It gave me purpose during a really sad time. Because the truth was, I missed my fiancé. I missed my bonus kids. I missed my things and my house too. (Keep in mind that I had moved the contents of my eighteen-hundred-square-foot house to Florida, where most of my earthly possessions still were.) But I didn't know where to begin to repair our relationship. And I didn't even know if he wanted to repair it. Four whole weeks had gone by, and we hadn't spoken. Our only communication was a few short and to-the-point texts. I was so lost about the way forward. Should I begin a new life on my own or try and repair the one I had?

Just before I left for my second speaking engagement of the year, I spoke to a little old lady about an apartment behind her house that was for rent. I remember my stomach rumbling with anxiety after I hung up. A lease is a pretty permanent thing. Just then, God whispered to me, "Talk to him [my fiancé]. You at least owe him that."

So with my fingers shaking, I sent him a text, "Can we talk?"

We arranged to speak that evening on the way to my speaking engagement in Baton Rouge. I pulled into the hotel, a big ball of nerves, literally shaking as I got my key from the front desk. I mean, here it was, the rest of my life. There was either a way forward or there wasn't. This was that defining moment.

WOOSAH!

When he called I answered with a shaky voice. The confidence in our relationship was gone. I was at ground zero, broken, gutted. I was either leaving this conversation a single woman or there was a path to reconciliation. I began first:

"I think we forgot how to be best friends."

"I agree."

"We hurt each other a lot."

"You left me."

"You told me to leave."

Before we could continue any further with the blame game—which we often play as frail humans—I desperately lassoed the conversation back to a gentle, healing place. Stuff like, "How are you?

No really, how are you?" Then I hit him with how the Lord had been convicting me in the weeks away from him and my bonus kids. My own sin.

Our Papa God had been sending people to minister to my sin in the most loving way. He sent my friend Morielle who is more like a little sister. In January 2021, I was having a phone conversation with her just ahead of her wedding that spring. I knew she and her husband, Jordan, were honoring God by waiting until marriage to be physically intimate. She didn't utter a word of condemnation; she didn't have to. Her obedience shone so brightly that it lit up my sin. I babbled to her about how Christopher and I were going to be married and that God knew he was going to be my husband. I was trying to rationalize playing house and sharing a bed with someone who was not my husband. I knew it was wrong, plain and simple.

I distinctly remember my brother Matthew pouring into me as well, but he was more pointed, more big-brotherly. "That's not right, sis," he said. "God will not honor that."

So all of that was on my heart and my brain as I uttered quite possibly one of the most courageous sentences I've ever spoken.

"Christopher, I want you to know that whoever I end up with I will begin again and remain pure until the day I get married."

I said it with a rushing wind kind of power coming out of the deepest part of my soul and heart. That kind of bold obedience when you have messed up so badly is breathtaking.

Quite literally, the words took my breath away.

I do think we get glimpses of what we'll feel like in heaven in this lifetime. This was one of those moments for me. A moment when I was completely and wholly aligned with the will of God in my life, even when the world screamed an entirely different message. I held my breath, heart pounding out of my chest to hear his answer.

"I want that too," he said.

There it was, he was totally sold out to God, and his obedience mirrored mine. Wow.

I wish I could tell you that it was poof, magical, and we were back together, but that wasn't our story. Frankly, I wish more people would tell you "the rest of the story," as the famed radio host Paul Harvey used to say. I think we are suffocating the life and potential out of relationships because they don't measure up to what we have been taught the ideal relationship should look like. And social media is the lighter fluid to this problem. Comparison is sucking the joy out of us. I wish more people had told me relationships are hard. They aren't a Disney movie, and no knight is coming to rescue you. You gotta do the work, plain and simple. You gotta get your shovel, meaning you have to do the work, king, queen, royal.

After we hung up the phone, I called my brother Matthew. I told him what Chris had said to me. He let out a big whooping holler over the phone all the way from the Dominican Republic. That's the relentless joy in radical obedience.

That night as I got ready for bed, I remember feeling the Lord's presence so acutely, in a way I hadn't in some time, and it was then I realized just how big of a wedge sin had placed between me and God. I prayed, I read my Bible, I went to church, even. But I was living in sin, and that sin caused me to hide from God, to turn away from Him and His will for my life. Once I decided to rededicate myself to that obedience, the wedge was gone. I couldn't stop crying that night. Tears of joy. Tears of release. Tears of peace. No more justifying. I was right where I needed to be. I slept like a baby that night, soundly and deeply, better than I'd slept in a looonggg time.

I want to invite you to apply my story to your life right now. Is there a place in your life where you could rededicate yourself to obedience? A place where sin has placed a wedge between you and God?

Is there a time in your life when you can clearly look back and see that you tried to be your own crossing guard and failed? Write in the margins or the journaling space. This is your personal journal on joy, peace, faith, and YOU!

I drove back to Alabama after an amazing visit at LSU and got reacquainted with my sweet little basement apartment. I gave thanks again to my hosts and all the inanimate objects I had fallen in love with. Just a few days before, I had been trying to rush my healing, make things happen, and get ahead of God. But I wasn't supposed to be looking for an apartment. My best friend told me wholeheartedly I could stay as long as I wanted. I can still hear her precious words: "As long as Tate and I have a home, so do you." Talk about pulling your heartstrings. (I am beyond blessed in the friendship department.)

But what I love about God is that He is already there, ready to meet us in our missteps. I do not believe it was time to get an apartment, but it did give Christopher and me the opportunity to have a discussion we desperately needed to have. I am reminded of Romans 8:28: "And we know that God causes everything to work together for the good of those who love God and are called according to his purpose for them" (NLT).

Let me stop to remind you right now that you are not too far gone, too messed up, or too defective. Those are the lies of the enemy. If you are still breathing, there is time to get it right. You picked up this book on purpose. There is no word for coincidence in the Hebrew language. This message is for you.

Not long after I got back to Alabama, I went home to my mama's house just down the road (that's what we say about any distance one to fifteen minutes away in the South). It was on that ride down the road, with the first bit of spring traipsing through the air like a formerly pent-up child, that it hit me. I was the prodigal daughter, and I had come home. Home to my hometown, home to heal, home to where I should've gone all along before marrying Christopher. Home to where if my mama were alive, I would surely be.

I don't know if anyone else has a mama that can assert their will like an absolute boss, but my mama once took me out of a well-known bar in Alabama, the FloraBama, in my broken days by pinching me under the arm and whispering in my ear, "I brought you into this world; I can take you out," all while smiling sweetly and demurely at everyone else around us. Needless to say, I left the bar that day. And I needed to.

When she died, I lost my North Star. I lost my way. I had never lived with a man before Christopher, and the plan was for me not to until I was married. But just like the prodigal son in Scripture, coming home wasn't full of condemnation, lectures, or pain. Our heavenly Father had a robe and ring for me. He was planning a party. A party because I came home, repented of my sins, and got out of the pigsty. That's the Jesus I want you to know. The one who threw me a coming-home party.

I got out at my mama's log house that she and my stepdaddy had built log by log with love. The air smelled different. I was walking differently with this realization: I was supposed to be here all along. Her giant gardenias were beginning to bloom. Tears filled my eyes and a peace beyond understanding washed over me. Despite all my choices to do it my way, God had a plan for me still. And it was beautiful. It was yes and amen! And surely my mommy, grandmother, daddycakes, and all my people were rejoicing in heaven. I didn't grow up thinking I would be like a character straight from the Bible, but here I was.

I wonder if you can recall a time when you wandered far from God? Did you come back or are you still wandering? Is there still a wedge there?

Take it from me, COME HOME, my precious friend.

There is a robe and a ring waiting on you. He's prepared the greatest BBQ and party just for you, in your honor.

I believe in you; I know you have the courage to do what it takes to come home, even from the fetal position. Because Lord knows I have been there. I'm holding space for you as you read this. Believe me, I have prayed for you, precious reader (and friend), before there was even a book.

Take that first step, as hard as it might be, because it's the first step home.

I think this is a good point to take a break and ask yourself if there is anything you need to forgive yourself for. Oftentimes, feelings of shame and unworthiness will keep us bound and believing that we aren't deserving of forgiveness ourselves. Forgive others? I can work on that. Forgive me? Oh, no! It's time to throw off the chains of that lie and start to believe, in the deepest part of your marrow, that you, my friend, are worthy of forgiveness.

I also share with people a lot that forgiveness is often a process. Once you say those words and grant that grace to yourself or another human being, it might take time to work its way through all of your being. You might have to say it over and over again for many moons—and continue to process the wrongdoing—until your heart and soul catch up with your brain. And that is A-okay, my love. Forgiveness is not a linear process. And no two people's forgiveness journey looks the same. I have forgiven in some radical situations where the world definitely told me not to, and the results were and are astounding.

I am living relentlessly in joy because I chose to forgive myself. I am living with relentless joy because I chose to forgive others. And I have to keep choosing forgiveness every day. But in that, I am actually choosing freedom. Will you join me in choosing the freedom of forgiveness?

JOYSTART

Spend some time journaling and/or praying about the following questions: Is there something in your life that is creating a wedge between you and God? What steps can you take to remove that wedge? Is there a particular sin you are justifying? Do you need to forgive yourself or someone else?

Do you have a north star? Are they still living? If so, could you call or write them and tell them thank you for guiding you? If they are passed on like mine, don't be afraid to talk to them or write a letter. Sometimes just the act of putting words on paper is so cathartic.

CHAPTER 8

The Power of Vulnerability

I n 2015, I had the most beautiful encounter with Dak Prescott, the current Dallas Cowboys quarterback. His beloved mother, Peggy, passed after roughly a year-and-a-half battle with cancer while he was playing quarterback at Mississippi State. I visited with Dak in the fall in Starkville, only forty-two days after my own father passed away unexpectedly.

I remember fighting for the assignment to cover Dak. I told my editors at the large media company I was freelancing for that I had a hunch about this kid, about State's season, to trust me. They did, finally, after a lot of pleading, and off we went: me, my amazing makeup gal and friend, Ginger, a ton of exquisite equipment, and two producers from New York. We flew around a tornado—a real tornado—and landed in Birmingham, Alabama, before driving three hours to get to Starkville, Mississippi. We arrived in the very wee hours of the morning.

I had done my research on Dak and his mama and knew how precious the bond was that these two shared. She loved all of her sons, but she doted on Dak the most.

I, too, know what it feels like to be the apple of someone's eye.

I was my daddy's only child.

He chose me, literally.

He fell in love with my mama, and then he fell in love with me. At eighteen months old, he gave me his last name and his life. And at that moment, he became mine, and I was forever his little girl. I still am today. I also learned about the power of adoption—the all-encompassing, life-changing, family-making power of adoption.

Going into the interview, Dak and I connected on another level as well, in a way that I don't wish for anyone else. We are part of the unenviable club of losing a parent far sooner than they are supposed to go.

Did I mention that I really, really hate cancer?

While the producers set up lights and cameras, Dak and I just walked and talked. I could barely contain my tears. I was still really raw from losing my father. Dak knew that instinctively. He looked beyond my tears to see Rachel the person, not Rachel the reporter. That touched me greatly. I've seen him several times since and have tried to explain what his intuitive knowing meant to me, but I'm not sure that I've ever been able to fully articulate how being seen that day—really seen—impacted me.

I sincerely hope this book and chapter convey my deepest gratitude.

Once we finally sat down for the interview, we talked about expectations, State's upcoming game, his coach Dan Mullen, and his mother, Peggy. We bonded over our love of tattoos. We both have tattoos to honor our parents on the inside of our wrists. His reads "MOM," honoring his mother and standing for "mind over matter," as he would later tell me.

He said, "That was her way, even in the face of that terrible disease. She rarely complained. So how can I complain?"

During the interview there were times we both got misty-eyed, but there was also laughter and joy. I felt Peggy and my father, David, all around us. Dak talked about managing expectations and smiled at the Heisman trophy talk (given to the most outstanding player in college football; Dak was a front-runner). He wouldn't stay on that topic though. He was more anxious to talk about his team and his Peggy. (What a guy!)

"I could tell her anything and she would tell me anything," he said. "She was my best friend. What she taught me, I want to portray to the world."

Dak's connection to his mother was apparent even from an early age. When he was ten, Peggy didn't have enough money for Christmas. She promised her boys that when her income tax check came in, they would have Christmas. In the meantime, she handed each one of her boys a hundred-dollar bill. Off they went to the mall to pick up their Christmas wares, but instead of spending the money on himself, ten-year-old Dak came back with a fancy makeup set and mirror for his mom. According to family, friends, teammates, and coaches, that's just who Dak is.

They all echo the sentiment of Dak's uncle, Philip Ebarb. "He's just that special."

Ebarb shared a rather poignant story with me involving Dak facing racism in the Deep South. "I've seen him change racism with the touch of his hand, literally," his uncle proclaimed. At the time of the incident, Ebarb was holding his nephew as they walked the halls of a hospital. Dak was four and receiving breathing treatment for asthma. A lady exited a hospital room, looked at the two (a white man carrying a black child), and gave an audible groan of disgust. Ebarb and Dak kept walking.

On their way back, they encountered the same woman. Dak, walking now, reached his chubby little hand up for hers. Reflexively she went to jerk her hand away from little Dak when he looked up and said, "Hi!"

"The lady literally melted, as if touched by God," his uncle recounted. "What a precious child."

Yep, that's Dak. To those who knew him before he was the quarterback of America's team, it was clear that he was always destined to be a superstar, a movie star, or someone very, very special.

Ebarb sends Dak text messages before and after each game, some reading, "It's just a game you're really good at. Relax, have fun and play the game. Stay humble." Or, "What would Mama do? What would Mama say? WWMS?"

I can say from experience that, like his mother before him, whatever Dak does or says is guided by humility and selflessness. Thank you, Dak, for reminding us all what goodness looks like in college football. And thank you for making an indelible mark on my life that day. Thank you for comforting my grieving spirit with your mere presence. In a world where we are constantly inundated with negative news, you are refreshing, you are what's right in this world, you are needed, and yes, you are special, Dakota Prescott.

You make your mama proud.

You make us all proud.

I wrote this piece, and week after week, it was one of the most read articles for the sports website I wrote for. When people searched for Dak, they found the article. (And lots of people search for Dak; I mean, he's the QB of America's team!) People wanted to know more about Dak personally, so the article continued to be read and got clicks galore through his early tenure with the Cowboys. The sports website it was published on is long since defunct, which is why I can share this with you in this book. (One reason I don't delete emails, my peeps!) And even though I'm no longer sportscasting, to this day, this assignment, this story, is still one of my absolute favorites.

It just goes to show you the absolute soul-shaking power of vulnerability. It took us both baring our souls to have this interaction and for this story to come about.

And here is the story of vulnerability behind the story. Before the article was published, I said to my sports website editor, "I recently interviewed Dak for another outlet. I would like to write a piece on him and his mother. We had a really amazing few moments suspended in time and they were really impactful to me, but no one cares about my personal story with him that day."

I said this. I actually said this out loud. And sadly, I truly believed it. After a lifetime of trying to shrink myself because people often told me I was "too much," I found myself slipping back into old patterns, trying to make myself smaller.

I want you to pause for a moment here and consider what message the broken world or broken people have told you throughout your life.

Here are a few common falsehoods I hear a lot:

You are too much.

You are not enough.

You are too emotional.

You are too reserved, uptight, shy, or quiet. (Why don't you talk more, loosen up?)

You are too stupid to do that.

You don't have what it takes to cut it.

You are unqualified. Good luck with that.

You will never achieve your dreams.

It was at this moment, in the face of my own insecurity, that my editor, Chadd Scott, said, "Yes, they do care. Your personal story will actually make this story different from all the other pieces on Dak Prescott."

I remember almost falling out of my dad's treasured recliner when he said that. He likely had no idea of the impact his words had on me, but he gave me permission to also tell my story in the article. But it was SO much bigger than that. He was talking about an article, but in reality, his words gave me the "attagirl" I needed to know that my story mattered too. I wasn't an award-winning quarterback but people wanted to hear about me, my experiences, and what I have learned.

And so, in turn, I will give you what Chadd Scott gave to me: YOUR STORY MATTERS TOO! You don't have to be famous in any measure, my dear.

YOU ALREADY MATTER!

His simple instruction to also tell my story was an immeasurable gift wrapped in a seemingly mundane work conversation. And oh boy, when I unwrapped that gift, I found an invitation to stop shrinking and walk in all my glory.

Here's what I know: my boss never would have said these words to me if I hadn't gotten vulnerable first and told him what I was really thinking—"No one wants to hear my story." Looking back, I can see how all of this was born from radical vulnerability.

True transformation requires bold vulnerability.

True transformation requires bold vulnerability. That is the cost.

I once heard Pastor Jentezen Franklin preach on gifts that are wrapped in unexpected packages. He said we often don't open these precious gifts because they aren't what we want or expect wrapping-wise. In some hoity-toity circles, the gift is often shunned because it's not properly wrapped. What a shame. I wonder how many gifts we don't open because we just don't take the time to investigate further. Maybe they are ugly on the outside. Or maybe we don't slow down to sit with the gift (busybodies unite!) or take the time to see how it makes us feel. Or maybe the gift doesn't speak our language or look like us, or maybe the gift makes us uncomfortable. Maybe the gift is smelly or dirty.

In #ImChangingtheNarrative, we call it taking off your mask, or radical vulnerability, as you have heard me say.

Imagine what beautiful gifts await us and those around us when we let the world see all of us, see what is behind the mask.

In the same vein, I know that the amazing interaction with Dak would not have happened if I hadn't fessed up to my enormous grief, if I hadn't shared how raw I was at that very moment. I could have said, "I am fine," and scurried away to my makeup artist to powder my red face. But I didn't. That magic interview, and bonding over the loss of our parents, would've never happened if I had kept myself hidden.

This is your invitation, today, to stop hiding who you are! The world needs you in all your glory.

I still remember the sports information director commenting to me just after the interview, "I've only seen him open up like that to Tom Rinaldi." (Tom is one of the GOATs of storytelling.)

I looked at him and said, "Well, we are both members of an awful club, one I wouldn't wish on another living soul."

Again, we are members of the lost-our-parents-too-young club. While I wish, desperately, that Dak and I still had our mothers (mine would pass four short years later)—and I certainly wish I had my daddycakes—the Lord brought beauty from what was left in ashes. And isn't that all we can really ask for, beauty from ashes in this broken world?

I truly believe the key to that heavenly exchange is vulnerability. There are soul gifts and stories that are just waiting to be unwrapped, but again it will cost you something. It does require your radical vulnerability.

But that's the catch-22 of vulnerability, right? We all desperately want to be seen and loved for who we truly are, but we also fear that if we are fully known, we'll be unlovable. That's what makes true vulnerability so scary. It means we have to open up. We have to show our truest self and risk rejection.

But can I tell you something, friends? God will never reject you. He sees you—I mean ALL of you—and loves you more than you could ever imagine. And when you are vulnerable with Him, He will prove to you just how lovable you truly are.

If we know we are going to hurt, if we know we cannot avoid pain in this life, then all we can really do is truly hold our seemingly mundane gifts, shake them, investigate them, and take the time to see how they make us feel and what we discover about ourselves in the process. And while you're doing it, my dear, I double-dog dare you to be you—in all your glory and brokenness. I've often heard that a disco ball is hundreds of pieces of broken glass put together to make a magical ball of light.

"HONEY, YOU'RE NOT BROKEN; YOU ARE A DISCO BALL!"

If you employ this removal of the mask in your own life, you will start to look at conversations differently, you will sleep differently, and you will walk and talk differently. This won't happen overnight; it will take you a lifetime to continually prime yourself to walk in this lane, in this light. Oh, but my dear, that's where the living is!

I will scream this from the rooftops till the day I go to be with my Maker: I am alive in a way that I have never been before because I chose to walk in all my glory, and that includes the good and the bad.

Do I still find myself in the middle of telling a story that I wish I would've never started? Feeling like I said too much? Like I know someone isn't tracking with me or doesn't get me or my story?

Yep. You bet I do! All the time, in fact! But what I can take from those experiences is maybe, just maybe, I showed someone else how to be vulnerable, how to fumble and bumble but still be beautifully open!

And for that, I'll never feel an ounce of regret.

Can you think of a time when God delivered you a beautiful gift that was wrapped in a mundane or boring package?

What would it look like this week, this month, this day, to let people see you, really see you? What would it look like to start having deeper conversations? To slough away the ordinary in order to see the real and the new?

If you are shaking your head at me right now and saying it's simply not possible, let me share another story. I recently took my husband away for a staycation near our home. We needed some *us* time. If you are otherwise attached, I know you can relate. We both work, and he has four amazing, beautiful, wonderful kids who gave me the title "Bonus Mom." They are all active, so they keep us really busy beyond our work.

Oftentimes, that leaves us little time for each other, so this particular weekend was *really* needed. While he coached flag football for our son that Friday night, I arrived early at the Cape Cod–style inn nestled on the beach on Amelia Island. I set up our room with mementos that reminded us of our past. Then I sat on the shared porch overlooking the ocean, and I wrote parts of this book.

In the short time I was there, I made friends with Craig, who worked behind the front desk. He was so helpful and anticipated anything I needed as I waited for my husband to arrive later that evening. It didn't take long for us to begin to chat on a deeper level. We both shared that we had lost our precious mothers to breast cancer. His mama was gone within days of her diagnosis. Mine was gone in ten months.

Time and time again, I find that there is common ground if we are only willing to go there. If we are willing to take off our masks. That sacred ground is all around us if we are open to these sorts of things. Let my words be a reminder to you to be radically open. These everyday miracles, as I call them, are everywhere, just waiting to be noticed, waiting to be experienced.

At that moment, just like with Dak, Craig and I forged a bond. Before the weekend's end, I had several more of these blessed encounters. I'd like to think it was the magical mix of Jesus, salt air, and the melodies of Jimmy Buffett playing in my mind.

The next morning, I sent my husband for an acupuncture appointment and made a beeline for the oceanfront porch once again to write. I noticed a sweet old lady rocking in the chair in front of the table I was typing away at. I admired her and pondered for a moment about her life.

I often do this with people and places. I'll drive by a house and wonder: Who lives there? Are they happy? What have they survived that was meant to kill them? What have those walls seen? And the older the home, the better. I've done U-turns just to take pics of old homes that called out to me.

Anyway, I watched the little old lady as she gazed out on the ocean. She brought me great peace without ever even knowing it. (I hope I do the same in people when it comes to stirring up passion, kindness, and purpose.) Not long after, she went to get up but couldn't quite get enough momentum to get her tushy up from the deep rocking chair. I watched, not wanting to impede on her dignity, but when she silently tried again to no avail, I sprang into action.

I stepped up, asking with a murmur if I could help her, and gently put out my arm. I didn't want her to think I was some weirdo sitting behind her and studying her every move, even though that's exactly what I was doing. (Sidenote: Can we all just start a harmless, the-good-kind-of-weirdo group and meet online or something? I need you, my peeps!) I hoisted her up as she gazed at me. Her simple and thankful look made me feel like I had won a soul Emmy or something, people. It was that special. I held the door for her to go inside and we exchanged smiles from our hearts, and away she went.

I went and sat back down feeling really proud of who my people raised me to be, when a man who was also on the porch came up and said, "I feel so bad. I didn't see she needed help until you were already there."

I patted him on the arm assuredly and said, "It's okay, I promise! I just happened to be right behind her and noticed."

'Cause that's the thing. If we open our eyes to look for simple ways to extend kindness to others, we will notice opportunities all around us. Yes, it will take putting yourself out there, and yes, that can be vulnerable. But I think you will be surprised as to how this little practice of noticing impacts the joy you experience in your own life.

And one last story about Dak Prescott. After fighting so hard for that interview, I got there that morning and found all the cameras facing toward him. I fully recognize my role as a reporter. The story isn't about me; I'm just the conduit. But I would've loved to be included after pushing so hard to make the interview happen. I was sitting across from him, in close proximity, trying not to cry and figuring out how to advocate for myself. I had just worked up the courage to ask about the cameras when Dak noticed what was going on. He asked the producer if one camera could be on me so that I could be included. They obliged.

Be a Dak. Be a noticer. Be a watcher. Take off your mask and let people see the real you. And fight for people while you are at it. I can't wait to hear how your life is radically changed when you do this.

JOYSTART

Could you make a pact with yourself to be a diligent watcher too? Could you be a noticer? Could you take off your mask and make those radical connections?

In the margins or journaling space, write about a time you did just that. How did it make you feel? What do you think makes it difficult for you to take off your mask? Where is your mind when you are not noticing others? How can you start a discipline of watching for others today? Once you do, I bet you end up feeling pretty amazing. And I bet there is even a soul Emmy with your name on it too. But if not, I know we made God proud, and truth be told, that is better than any earthly award. Because here's what I know: earthly treasures will rot and fade away, so let us work for treasures in heaven.

> Do not store up for yourselves treasures on earth, where moths and vermin destroy, and where thieves break in and steal. But store up for yourselves treasures in heaven, where moths and vermin do not destroy, and where thieves do not break in and steal. For where your treasure is, there your heart will be also. (Matt. 6:19–21)

CHAPTER 9

Feed Your Soul

When the pandemic hit in early 2020 and the world was forced to lock down, every speaking engagement I had booked through the fall was canceled within two weeks. As each call came in, I was more and more despondent. This was my livelihood; I created the whole movement, #ImChanging theNarrative, from scratch, from nothing. The movement, my baby, existed fiscally because of my speaking engagements. Now it seemed as if what I had spent the last four years building was all in jeopardy!

I broke down and cried my eyeballs out in my home in Nashville as one of the last calls from the planned gigs came in and said, "Our hands are tied. Our funds have been frozen. Let's just stay in touch."

I had gotten many variations of this same message all week. I stayed in bed for an extended period of time. I had just retired from sportscasting the previous fall, after hosting the first mental health game between two Big Ten (collegiate sports conference) college football teams. During the lockdown, while all these rejections were coming in, I was busy shaking my fist at God. I questioned Him. I groaned. I cried. And I cried some more. And boy, did I look back. In fact, I looked back so much that I should've turned into a pillar of salt in these modern times. (Just a joke, comparing myself to Lot's wife fleeing Sodom and Gomorrah in Genesis 19:17, 26: "One of them said, 'Flee for your lives! Don't look back, and don't stop anywhere in the plain! Flee to the mountains or you will be swept away!' . . . But Lot's wife looked back, and she became a pillar of salt.")

If we are being really honest with one another, I think there are times when we have all shaken our (collective) fists at God and looked back into a dying land. It could be because of a relationship or job that we long for even though it is toxic; it could be because of the death of a loved one or people around us who are having babies when we are unable. Whatever it is, most of us would agree that as humans it is easy to look back and long for "better days" or wish for our lives to be different. There are times in which we have all questioned the sovereignty of the almighty God or just questioned life itself.

It's human nature to question, but know that God can handle our fists, our rebellion, and our questions. He loved us from the very beginning of time so much that He gave us free will. He could have created us to obey Him, love Him, to *have to* serve Him, but instead He gave us the option to choose Him or not choose Him. I think that's so rad. To put it simply, *we* get to choose Him the same way He chooses us.

Unfortunately, I know that many people don't choose God, and that breaks His heart. Maybe you're a seasoned believer or maybe you're not familiar with His infinite love and the Scriptures. Either way, let me remind you of this beautiful truth: "'For I know the plans I have for you,' declares the LORD, 'plans to prosper you and not to harm you, plans to give you hope and a future'" (Jer. 29:11).

I have seen His plans play out in my life over and over again. I can see when He has doted on me, sent me *love letters* or *God winks*. I can see where I was going to take a left but instead followed Him to the right and ended up far better off than I could have ever imagined. God's desire isn't to control us but to lead us to His good plans for us. Choosing God's way is choosing what is ultimately best for ourselves and best for those around us. It is choosing to care for ourselves like the miracles we are.

It breaks God's heart when we don't value and recognize ourselves as miracles. God did not take the day off when He made you. Let me repeat that: God was not out to lunch at the heavenly branch of Panera the day you were created. (Come on now, you know that bread is otherworldly.) He knew you before you were knitted in your mother's womb. He not only knows the number of hairs on your head, but He knows their order. You aren't defective and you are not broken, my dear. I tell people this all of the time: the same loving Creator who thought the world needed the Andes and Kilimanjaro, lovingly thought the world could also use one of you.

You do not need to be sent back to the factory for reassembly. Trust me on this.

And here's the coolest part: no one on this planet can accomplish what you were sent to accomplish. There is a beautiful and one-of-a-kind road map associated with your fingerprints and your heartbeat. You have things, places, and people that are uniquely assigned to you. For example, I believe I was born to create #ImChanging theNarrative, to put my unique stamp on it, to use my experiences to help others. That's what I am hoping for you. There are people you haven't met yet whom you are going to love, and there are times you're not yet aware of when you will be sent into a situation specifically for someone. You are their angel, their guidepost. And the beautiful part is you may or may not ever know this side of heaven the vast impact you will have in this lifetime.

There is a beautiful and one-of-a-kind road map associated with your fingerprints and your heartbeat.

But you do need to learn to love, care for, and value yourself. You need to learn how to care for your soul, which is deeper than self-care. (That's why we call it soul care!)

When we were all collectively locked down, we were being inundated with horrific news 24/7. You couldn't escape it. We heard it from friends on the phone and via texts from our families and coworkers. The television carried so much sad news. And don't even get me started on social media. No one knew much, and what they did know was bad news. If you listened to the news all day, it was enough to put you in a funk so deep that it felt like you were at the bottom of a dark well with no way out.

Do you feel me?

I have always had some notion of what fills my cup, but I had never studied soul care as I did during the lockdown. Having been diagnosed with clinical depression just the year before in 2019, I really had to work to take care of myself in isolation. I had to learn where, when, and how. I became a course study of Rachel Joy Baribeau. I was the student, the instructor, and the dean overseeing the class. The only other earth-side attendee was my therapy dog, Buddy Jo Baribeau.

After all those gigs canceled on me, I really wanted to throw in the towel—and I was this close to doing it, I tell ya. But then I heard the voice of God. For me, it's not a voice booming down from the heavens like in the movie *The Ten Commandments* with Charlton Heston. It is an actual voice I hear in my spirit. It is unmistakably Him.

While I was in two-day-old bedclothes and crying in my sheets, I heard Him ask, "Do people need you?"

"Yes, God."

"Do they need you now more than ever?"

"Yep. So much. People are really hurting."

"Can you reach them?"

"Yes, Lord, I can. The internet can be a beautiful place. And I'm thankful for technology like Zoom."

"Have I given you a specific set of gifts and talents to be able to reach them?"

"You know it, Lord. I am so grateful."

"Do you have a story of overcoming? Can you tell them how I helped you?"

114

"I will scream it from the rooftops. Thank you for saving me." After this conversation with God Almighty, I threw those covers back like I was throwing off a wet blanket of despair. I put my feet on the ground with a renewed sense of purpose. I had a plan. I had my fire back!

We (the people who make the music play behind the scenes at my movement, aka my dream team) began to call every school we had ever been to and new schools and people we had never met, and we offered our services. Mostly for free because, again, most people's budgets were frozen.

I threw myself into studying. I took courses on happiness; I read every article on coping I could get my hands on. I studied self-care and I studied fear. I studied courage. I listened to many other speakers. I listened to God.

I stayed outside in my backyard as much as possible, soaking up the spring sun. I bought a used firepit and some firewood. I planted a raised-bed garden full of ancestral corn. (I'm Mayan and corn is a big deal in my culture.) I planted celery and later juiced the celery I grew. Talk about satisfaction. I stood out under the stars at night contemplating life. I leaned into my neighbors Allison, Jake, and Brittany (and her babies) and loved them even harder, as we pulled together and created a buddy system for the grocery store and whatnot.

I learned how much bad news I could take and when. I started to look at my soul as an ecosystem. Junk in and I'm polluting my ecosystem. And junk could be crappy food, people who kill your dreams, toxins, negative self-talk, and even crime shows, my guilty pleasure. I'm interested in true crime because I'm fascinated by why people do what they do. I was mindful not to watch, listen to, or read true crime articles, shows, or stories late at night, lest I have horrific nightmares.

And the same goes for the good stuff going into my soul's ecosystem. Sunshine, Jesus, burning firewood, flowers, homegrown produce, helping others, connecting with other humans, exercise, dancing, learning new things, and prayer were some of the things that helped beautify my soul during such a tenuous time. I also learned that *The Office* (a silly, politically incorrect TV show about an office led by a bungling and inappropriate boss) was one of the greatest forms of self-care for my own soul.

There were days I had a ton of things on my to-do list, but I just couldn't do them. I was in a funky place a decent amount of the time, still processing the loss of my mother and my income, and I was still battling depression. I had learned the value of checking in with myself daily from our resident psychologist at #ImChanging theNarrative, Dr. Joshua Klapow. On days that were just plain hard, I would go from my bed to my daddy's beloved recliner, and I would teleport to Scranton, Pennsylvania, and Dunder Mifflin (the location and fictional name of *The Office*). It was my escape. It was stupid and silly, but it worked.

What is silly and stupid but makes you happy? What if we collectively stopped worrying about looking silly and cared more about what feeds our souls? How happy and full we all might be! Woo-wee, that'll preach! I imagine there would be fewer people barking at the cashier in the grocery store line and flipping people off in traffic. Because just like hurt people hurt people, so do healed (or healing) people heal people.

Here's what I know for certain: you've gotta be doggedly determined in finding what works for you, my love. And it also bears repeating that we are all so uniquely different. What fills your cup doesn't cut it for me and vice versa. I teach people in my talks, and it's my honor to teach you this now: you have to start looking at yourself as the ultimate experiment and do it for the rest of your ever-loving life.

You are so worth it. You are a masterpiece. As Scripture reminds us, "We are God's handiwork, created in Christ Jesus to do good works, which God prepared in advance for us to do" (Eph. 2:10).

I can't speak with any authority except as someone who should have tapped out multiple times but didn't. But I can say this with conviction: I think it pains God to see us scurrying around down here, dry, flammable, hurting, bitter, and busy. His beautiful, precious masterpieces, broken and bleeding in a million pieces.

How do we fix this?

My friend Kayce Smith of Barstools Sports told me that she spends almost all of her time listening to sports, talking about sports, or talking to others about sports. She shrewdly said to me, "When am I supposed to hear my own thoughts, Rachel?" Because of her crazy schedule, she is intentional about getting completely silent—no music, no podcast, no nada. She simply cooks dinner, alone with her own thoughts. I have never forgotten that simple but astute advice.

When is the last time you got quiet and got really still?

Sometimes I love driving with no music, just me and my own thoughts. I will also incorporate the breathing exercise our resident mindfulness expert, Lindsay Freeman, taught us. Remember, six seconds of breathing in, hold for two seconds, and six seconds out. Repeat up to ten times. It is revolutionary for anxiety, stress, and infiltrating your body with oxygen. Crazy enough, but did you know that most people use only 20 percent of their lung capacity? It is remarkable that we only use a limited amount of our lungs. (And our brains too; there are parts of our brains we don't use or access.)

And did you know that 70 percent of toxic elimination from your body exits through breathing?[1] We are exposed to toxins every single day. Yes, the soul toxins we previously discussed but also everyday physical toxins from products, food, the air, and more. When we allow our bodies to carry toxins around like uninvited houseguests who have stayed too long, we are inviting all sorts of illness and disease. Get to breathing, sweet cheeks. Your health depends on it: mind, body, and spirit.

I've spoken to hundreds of coaches and have received follow-up emails from them saying things like how they know the concept of filling their cup of their own self-love is important. Some have felt good or relaxed, but now they're being deliberate in filling their own self-love cup. It's helping them be their best!

This is what I live for, what I work for, what I exist for, to help others start to radically love themselves in a way that is extraordinary beyond belief.

My mama used to say, "BBB." Blessed beyond belief.

What if we began to love ourselves and care for ourselves in a way that is blessed beyond belief? There are too many people walking around who have never even pondered self-care, or if they have, it's surface-level generic stuff. I get my nails done but I gotta tell you, my soul has never been nourished in a nail salon. It's just not deep enough. Just like getting a new haircut or hairdo. You look great, you feel great, and sometimes the cut/color is so great that you walk two feet taller. But I'm talking soul-deep stuff.

It's deeper than self-care. It's why we call it *soul care* in my movement.

Do a little thought experiment with me. Go back to your childhood and sit with your inner child, aka little you, when you first remember playing and giggling. What brought you joy? Did you take piano lessons but quit? Did you always dream of taking acting classes? Did you want to be a pastry chef? Do you have an idea or movement burning inside of you? One that will change the world for the better far after you are gone?

I had an amazing lash artist one time tell me she had a dream of starting a cat sanctuary but couldn't even see the first steps to make it happen, she was so engrossed with business. And rightfully so. If there is no income, you can't pursue your dreams. But in a short amount of time, we talked about training others in the lash industry, expanding her current studio, or working out of a home office. We also discussed her two-, five-, and ten-year plan. We broke it down into baby steps on how to get there. (Often, we get so frozen by the gigantic goal that we simply cannot make the first move. Let's get unstuck, together!)

Now, I couldn't see her because I had my eyelids taped back, but I could feel realization enter the room like the first time you turn on the heat in winter. It settled over both of us.

118

What would it look like to take yourself through a similar process, to map out how you want to see change in your life and how you will grow in prioritizing your own soul care? Write it down. Make a two-, five-, and ten-year plan, and list out the things that are going to help you get there. Now circle the things you already know are surefire ways to fill your cup. All of the others are to be considered the grand experiment of you. Maybe you want to try something totally new. Want to learn to hang glide or learn a new language or skill? (Hello, YouTube is your friend!) And let's take it one step further: What if you bought a poster and got your family, your roommate, and your partner in on the action? What if you all wrote down your goals and dreams and the small steps needed to get there? What if you talked about soul care together and held each other to it?

I know my husband is happier when he's napping, being silly with his kids, going to acupuncture, and getting proper rest. These are all things that fill his cup. I am cognizant of and vigilant about making these things happen for him. Get someone in your life who will be cognizant and vigilant about holding you to your soul care. It's time to start being deliberate in filling your own self-love cup.

The best possible version of you is waiting.

JOYSTART

Make a list of all the things that bring you pure joy. Maybe it's playing with your kids, journaling, praying, meditating, playing an instrument, taking a hike, going dancing, riding a bike, or snuggling with your fur-babies. Do you feel refreshed when you take a long bath or after going on a walk? Maybe it's learning a new skill or sitting in complete silence. List all the things you love and all the things you have dreamed of doing. Then create a two-, five-, and ten-year plan on how you are going to slowly incorporate some or all of these things into your life. Take a few pages of your journal just to dream, or use the journaling space in the back of this book.

CHAPTER 10

The Pity Kiddie Pool

Have you ever been with your family, at work with lots of people, or in a crowded room or bar and felt utterly and hopelessly alone?

I have.

I have many times.

And if this describes you, imagine me reaching through the pages of this book right now to give you a bear hug . . . holding you for at least twenty seconds. In fact, studies show that oxytocin, "also called the 'bonding hormone,' is a crucial feel-good hormone in the body. Research indicates that (1) it 'inspires the feeling of meaningful connection with others'; (2) it is 'also linked to reducing blood pressure and the risk of heart disease.' Some refer to it as the 'happy hormone.'"[1] Research has discovered that there is something magical to having long hugs. They have figured out that oxytocin is released when we hug for at least twenty seconds. In other words, a short, quick hug, like those at the church door, will not produce oxytocin.

I have been healed by a hug. I have felt seen in a hug. I have felt anxiety dissipate from my body through a hug. I have let go of anger with a hug. I have seen God reflected in the actions and love of people with a hug.

Yep, they are that powerful.

I want to hug you long enough to produce oxytocin. I want to step out of this book and heal you with a hug, help you let go of anger and anxiety and depression with a hug. I wish I could hug all your loneliness away, but sadly I can't. All I can do is share my own stories of loneliness and how they manifested into something far more beautiful, in hopes that you feel less alone.

And I cannot promise you that you won't feel lonely again because I think it's just part of our story, part of how a lot of us are made. For some of us, the aches cut just a bit deeper, and the thoughts twirl and swirl a little harder than most. Some of us can get really lost in our feelings. And I don't want you to beat yourself up. Being connected with your emotions is a huge blessing that a lot of people struggle to find! I just want you to make note of this, fellow over-feeler: you are not alone. I got that badge too at birth. It's on the invisible sash I wear that is draped across my chest.

But just as with pain, there is an invitation, I think, in loneliness if we are willing to go there. For a lot of my life, I wasn't willing. Instead, I just leaned into what I knew: triggers, old patterns, and false beliefs. Now I can see it for what it is and what it was.

The loneliness was a hand reaching out with an invitation—for better, for more, for different. And that hand belonged to Jesus.

I distinctly remember being lonely in a bar in Columbus, Georgia, in my late twenties. I was dressed to the nines, with a group of fun people, and shoulder to shoulder in a crowd, but I was achingly lonely. The feeling was so palpable that I had to gulp it down just to avoid choking on it. I turned in a circle to see if anyone else was witnessing this internal meltdown. This reckoning of my soul. No one was. It was all in my head, or was it? I think it was also in my heart and my cells and, of course, my soul. I even felt it in my toes.

Looking back, I know this like I know the sun will rise tomorrow: that utter feeling of aloneness had a gift wrapped in it (apparently a theme of my life). It was a hand outstretched telling me there was more, a different life, a different way of living. The loneliness was an invitation for better, for more, for different, and the hand belonged to Jesus. That's what I love about our Papa God. Even in my iniquity and my addiction, He never stopped calling to me.

I had a successful appearance on the outside but was smashed to smithereens on the inside. What had started as a little harmless experimentation (or so I thought) after the bar one night in college had turned into a full-blown addiction. I was using hard drugs multiple times per week. I had been a user for seven or eight years, my addiction steadily progressing throughout those years. I couldn't be social without it. I was using downers to sleep after an entire night and sometimes a morning of partying. It was a wonder my heart didn't cease to beat. I was hiding my stash from other friends that used in order to keep more for myself. And when there wasn't enough in my bank account to support my habit, I began to sell it to make sure I had what I needed.

In all of this iniquity, my God—our God—never stopped calling to me. I saw a vision of Him one night in the corner of my room. Instead of the "mad dad" look I expected, it was a brokenhearted, I-created-you-for more-than-this look.

"Come home," He beckoned.

My heart is verklempt just typing this. What love He has for us.

Not long after that, I attended a party on the lake near where I lived in Columbus. I had been really listening to God and leaning into the sinking feeling in the pit of my stomach that this was all going to end really badly if I didn't get clean. God had also given me a dream, a vision, and a warning—that I was a runaway train going the wrong way down the track, and if I didn't get clean, I was going to break my family's heart, kill someone else, end up in jail, or all of the above. He had my attention, but I thought it was just one last little hit of a hard drug. As soon as I took it, I began to bawl. Not the greatest reaction in a party scene.

I heard God whisper to me, "Your body is not your own anymore."

A friend that shall remain nameless was astute enough to see I was in a rough spot. He cleared people out of the guest room of this house and ushered me and my two sister Labradors into the room. (Yes, I brought my dogs to a party.) He made me lock the door so I could get some rest. It was Saturday night, late, but Sunday was coming, and I could not wait to get to church!

When I was fourteen, I was saved at a youth camp in Florida. At that camp, they were giving an altar call for anyone who wanted to accept the free salvation Jesus was offering. I was white-knuckling the pew, not humanly ready to fully give my little heart to the Lord. Although I had been in church my whole life, this time felt like it was for all the marbles. It felt like Jesus was asking for all of me. The only way to describe it is to say something supernaturally carried me down that aisle and thus began the greatest love affair I've ever known. But over the years, I still held back parts of myself—parts I was afraid to show anyone, let alone Jesus. Those hidden parts of me allowed a foothold for sin to slowly overtake me.

So here I was, adult Rachel, broken and so, so tired from doing it my way, trying to overcome an emptiness I was incapable of filling. An emptiness from my daddy issues that told me I was unworthy, unlovable, rejected, and abandoned. At the crack of dawn, I showered and drove so fast to church you could've mistaken me for Dale Earnhardt. My mom had recently been going to a sleepy mountain church called King's Pasture. As I wrote about in a previous chapter, this is where I heard the story of Joshua, the son of that church's pastor who was diagnosed with cancer. I was doing a story on him for my latest sportscasting reel. That morning I put my face on that carpeted altar and laid my addiction before me.

"Here are my most shattered bits, Lord," I prayed. "Can you take them and make them and me new?" The GOD of the universe supernaturally delivered me from a nasty and lengthy addiction.

When people ask me why I love the Lord so much, I tell them, "I should've been dead in a ditch ten times over, but He took me from the *gutter-most* to the *uttermost*." God used my loneliness as a lifeline to get my attention. It was like a check engine light for my soul. It was intricately tied to my addiction.

It may not be a drug addiction for you or your loved ones. It could be porn, food, gambling, shopping, sex, or alcohol. I know this: addiction is eating us alive as a society. And the more we try to hide it, the more the shame grows. Or maybe it isn't addiction at all but depression or anxiety crippling your joy. What is God trying to tell you in your loneliness?

The feeling of being utterly alone can happen anywhere—at a dinner table, with your family, or at work. I've been there. I have felt the sting of feeling invisible right smack-dab in the middle of a crowd.

I'm newly married. By the time this book comes out, I'll have been married for about a year and a half. My husband has kids. They are amazing kids. I'm talking out-of-this-world awesome kids. They gave me the title "Bonus Mom."

Our son Brooks is smart, smart. He can watch YouTube and fix anything. He is a warrior but also has a gentle heart.

Our daughter Leah is my brave girl, and once she knows what she wants, she is all in. She is just fourteen and is already working plus playing two sports. She and I have the same love languages— words of affirmation and gifts. I remind her all the time that she is a beautiful world changer, and I'm so proud of her.

Our third child, Beckham, is all boy. He loves NFL football and fishing. We bonded over our love of football. Once he had an eighty-three-yard TD return and was mad because he wanted more action in the game. Underneath that sports-loving exterior is a young man who feels deeply and is a protector by nature.

Libby is the baby. She makes us all laugh and keeps us on our toes. She reminded me to laugh again after my mommy passed. She is a worker bee and will be the CEO of a large company one day or will run the world. I kid you not.

While they gave me the gift of being called Bonus Mom, I am the clear winner here because I get to love them and learn from them daily. I'm obviously new at this mom thing and definitely experiencing some on-the-job training. Haha!

Recently, we were on the way to the gulf beaches for spring break, and I was just having a rough go of it. As much as my husband and these amazing kids include me, being a stepparent or bonus parent is tough. Let's call a spade a spade. Blended families are just plain hard. It's like they are part of this secret club, complete with supercool handshakes, and you, the bonus parent, are on the outside looking in a lot of the time. My tribe doesn't do it on purpose; they have just had all these memories and experiences together and a lifetime before me. It can make for an incredibly lonely place, just by the simple fact that you don't share DNA.

Not only that, but it's in these family moments that I miss my parents the most, when I'm doing something my parents taught me or loving in a way that is akin to the way they raised me. It's both beautiful and heartbreaking at the same time.

So here we are heading to the beach for spring break. It should be a happy, joyful time, but truth be told, I could not shake the loneliness or the grief. I felt utterly unreachable like I was lost somewhere down a long, dark hallway, unable to get back to the light of another human being. Almost to our beach destination, we made one last pit stop. Instead of going with everyone, I stayed in the car and began to cry. I didn't want to cry. I didn't want to make a scene or let my feelings influence them. I do my best not to burden them that way. I love them too much. But sometimes it just happens. We big-feeling people have rather large emotions.

I talked to God and my mommy in those few solitary moments in the car and pleaded for help from above with a guttural cry. I don't know about you, but there are many times I don't have the words to form a prayer. I feel that broken. So I cry out. I know He knows. I know God knows the language of my heart. I was so alone in my spirit, even in a packed car. Can you feel me? Ever been there? It was a doozy of a dark place to be.

As my family piled back in the car, so did the awkwardness. They knew I was upset. I had been quiet, and now I was trying to silently cry, but I'm a sniffler and puffy-faced crier. (And worse yet, my face swells the next day when I have cried a lot. Oh joy!) I had just cried out to God while they were in the store. And I knew this to be, once again, Him offering me a lifeline.

"Share your heart with them, Rachel," He whispered. "Share how you are feeling. They can't read your mind. They love you. Reach out to them instead of drowning in your grief and loneliness."

So that's what I did. I slowly started talking and commenting on the conversation in the car. I engaged. I was able to audibly express how I was feeling. I told them I was sad. I felt alone and I missed my people, badly. I even gave myself permission to laugh at their antics and silliness. Maybe it was part delirium from being in the car that long, but it felt good to feel something besides despair. And before I knew it, I wasn't so alone. I wasn't drowning anymore. Instead, I was gulping up goodness and laughter and innocence. I could see how God helped me to chase and choose the joy that was already all around me and in my heart because of the immense love I have for them, but it took me doing my part. I had to get that emotional shovel I always talk about and do the dang work. And when I say work, I mean take emotional action! Reach out, don't wallow in self-pity. Make a phone call, write an old-fashioned letter, send a text, hire a skywriter, send a carrier pigeon, but don't suffer alone.

My darling, there is no other way. You have to do the work. I have a hunch you already know this, and it's one of the reasons you picked up this book.

I teach about a concept the great women's college basketball coach Kay Yow shared: "Don't drown in self-pity. Swish your feet a little, then get out."[2] I like to think of that self-pity as a baby pool. We all have a baby "pity pool" in our lives. We live in a fallen world with sin, and we are not exempt from bad things happening to us. But some of us have taken up residence in our baby pool and are swimming laps in it. We've spent years being lonely, being miserable, wallowing in our misfortune. Feeling all the feels.

I'm going to preach to you as I preach to myself and like Kay Yow would preach to us all: SWISH YOUR FEET AND GET OUT!

You are going to be lonely; you are going to feel sorry for yourself. It's part of being human, but I am begging you not to stay there. I am begging you to swish your feet and GET OUT! You've spent too much time in that baby pool. I have as well at various times of my life. It's time to come out and live life to the fullest. I am here to tell you there is joy after the loneliness, there is joy after that misfortune. Heck, I'm even telling you there is joy in the midst of your loneliness and misfortune.

And my hope is that after reading this book, you are more open to it, that you actually do the work for your soul to be open to the joy and miracles that are everywhere around you, at this very moment, just waiting and begging to be recognized.

The next time you feel lonely I want you to recognize it. Name the feeling. Give it a name tag and a seat at the party. Write it down. Talk to the feeling, as silly as that may sound. Say it out loud, then don't be afraid to sit with it. I find hard feelings and memories have less power the more you sit with them and give them their due. I want you to imagine Jesus, with His beautiful nail-scarred hands, reaching out while you are drowning in said loneliness.

Now I want you to envision the baby pool. Can you see it? The pool of your problems? The unchanged water, murky and gross after years of being used. Now I want you to swish your feet and get out! Do you see yourself getting up, swishing the gunk from your feet, and getting out?

I do and boy, let me tell you, it's a powerful sight to behold!

This book is all about having a battle plan for your life. A literal plan to chase joy, to chase better, when life goes awry and crap hits the fan. Because inevitably we know it will.

Remember, we can choose bitter or we can be better, my love!
CHOOSE BETTER! Choose to chase joy relentlessly!

Many of the people I have worked with over the years have actually gotten Post-it notes and made themselves reminders of these affirmations, these truths, and they have stuck them on their mirrors, walls, dashboards, computer screens, or notebooks.

> *CHOOSE BETTER! Choose to chase joy relentlessly!*

In *A Million Miles in a Thousand Years*, Donald Miller writes about how we think we will remember our lives. He comments that

> the saddest thing about life is we don't remember half of it. Not even a tiny percentage, if you want to know the truth. I have this friend Bob (Goff) who writes down everything he remembers. If he remembers dropping ice cream on his lap when he was seven, he'll write it down. The last time I talked to Bob he had written more than 500 pages of memories.[3]

Let's be like Bob and Donald. Let's be proactive and capture our affirmations, our truths, our memories—yes, even our lonely times—so we can remember the hand that reached out to us to pull us from those dark times.

Because here's the rather sad alternative: we get some distance from a miracle, a joy, or even a hurt, and it fades into the recesses of our minds. Poof, gone. That's how fast-paced we are living. And don't even get me started on the amount of information and news we are bombarded with on a daily basis. "In the course of a day, the average person in a Western city is said to be exposed to as much data as someone in the 15th century would encounter in their entire life."[4]

These affirmations won't stick unless we make them stick! Let's make the stock of Post-it go up, beloved!

We've got work to do. Life is too precious to stay lonely, stay the same, or stay stagnant.

We ride at dawn!

In a time when you were lonely, have you ever felt God's hand reach down to save you? Psalm 18:16 says,

> He reached down from heaven and rescued me;
> he drew me out of deep waters. (NLT)

Or maybe you heard Him as I did in the car at the gas station. Maybe He came to you in your dreams or gave you a vision. Maybe He used another human being to help you out of your dark place. Maybe it was by an angelic encounter or through the love of a fur-baby. Whatever your unique story is, write it down. Document it for your grandkids and their grandkids.

God is worthy of it all!

But here is a hard truth, and there will be many in this book: He can't be the hero of your story if you don't acknowledge Him and His infinite goodness. Woo-wee, that'll preach.

Maybe you're reading this and you can't recall a hand reaching down to save you in your time of need, in your darkest, most alone moments. I can assure you that He was there, and He longs to be invited. You have to acknowledge Him. Why don't you try talking to Him right now? I can guarantee you He is ready and willing to listen. If this is your story, then I want you to look for His hand the next time you feel alone. Listen for the still, small voice.

And if you can't feel or hear God, speak first, even if you feel crazy. Trust me, I live part-time in Crazy Town. Many people in the Bible did too. He is there. I promise, boo! He is everywhere! He is just waiting to rescue you, to enter your story and make it better. He is waiting to attach purpose to your pain, just like He did for me. He is waiting to turn your loneliness into joy and your mess into a message! I am living proof, and all my days I will tell the world how he turned my desperate, lonely moments into a beautiful story of overcoming, connection, and sweet joy!

JOYSTART

Grab your pen and Post-it notes and turn to the blank journal space in this book. Start writing all the beautiful truths about yourself. Write them all. Write till your hand falls off. Now I want you to take a moment to mirror Bob Goff and start writing down your beautiful memories. Say you are at work when one comes to you and you can't get to this book. Use your notes app or voice memo until you get home and then transfer it when you are able. And remember to savor those memories when they bounce around the corners of your mind. Sit with them, notice their smell, their texture, the sound of them, and the essence of the memory. Soak in how it made you feel at the time it happened and how it makes you feel today. These memories are the very fabric of your story. Slow down and treasure them, sweet pea.

And lastly, because God is the true hero of our collective stories, I want you to document a time you felt lonely and His hand reached down to save you.

CHAPTER 11

My Father's Table

My father bought his large dining room table, I'm sure, with the hopes of having lots of souls around it and mouths just a waterin'. He was a chef after retiring from the military before going back into civil service. Cooking was his love language. But other than a guest here or there, holidays, or special occasions, his beautiful dining room table went unused except for him.

As his only child, every possession he owned went to me when he passed. And while I'm not about to be on the show *Hoarders*, I do like to keep things, a lot of things. In the months after he died, I hung on to his disposable spice containers like they were made of gold. I went to the store and bought new spices to put into the ones that came from his house. I needed to touch the things he touched. His property was the last remaining earthly connection I had to him, and a girl needs her daddy, always.

His beautiful dining room table came to find a place in my home. It was sacred and special and still is to this day. While we could certainly upgrade to something prettier and newer, it could not compare to the soul and the stories that this table has. In short, it's so much more than a table, but I digress.

I don't share the part about my dad being alone to disparage solitude or his memory but more so to say that I think we all buy or desire certain things in hopes of life turning out the way we want it to. The truth is, oftentimes it doesn't. Oftentimes, life just plain sucks.

That table would enter my home in Nashville, and immediately I began to host people for pots of tea around it. I began to have more and more people over for dinner and used that table. My young neighbor's baby would come over and color at that table. (She would later take her life due to bullying at the tender age of twelve.) I remember one of the first times my now-husband, Christopher, came to Nashville, and I cooked him a meal for one of our first dates. It was hamburger steak, asparagus, and cauliflower mashed potatoes using the same spices my daddy used and laying plates handed down from my grandmother on that precious table. And while Christopher never got to meet my father, there was a moment when I laid those plates down that it started to become clearer—not crystal clear but let's call it a tickle in my soul. My father's hands had touched the same places my future husband was touching while he was sitting at my father's table.

There have been pivotal times in my life when I knew but didn't really know just yet. Let me explain. Have you ever had a tickle in your soul? Maybe you haven't paid a ton of attention to your soul, and there is no judgment here if that's you. Maybe you've been coasting, surface-level living, or just barely hanging on and trying to survive, so you haven't had the time to get in touch with the innermost workings of your soul. And that is okay, but my hope is that after reading this book, you will become well acquainted and very much in tune with what your soul is trying to tell you.

Ring, ring, your soul is calling.

I knew back in 2014 that I would start #ImChangingtheNarrative, but I didn't see the problem yet, nor how I could be the solution. I just had a hunch. I felt the tickle that something rather large was coming. It's like being at the optometrist's office getting an eye exam. You can see those letters and numbers but they are still really fuzzy.

As my relationship with Christopher progressed over the years, I was always sad that he never got to meet my daddycakes. Never more so than when I prepared to get married. If ever two people would get along, it would be Christopher and my daddycakes. They are both veterans, *proud* military people, and both avid readers, well-studied on the art of war, politics, and football. Their temperaments are also very similar. I have often imagined what bringing Christopher home to my dad's house would've been like. I could have caught a catnap on the couch, as I often did, while my dad and my future husband gabbed in the kitchen about things that are wayyy above my paygrade! I'm people smart, feelings smart, art and history smart, but these two are genius-level smart.

Without fail, every time I left my dad's house, there was a daddy "sammich," as he called it, in a cooler with RC colas, a Whatchamacallit chocolate bar, and usually two frozen shepherd's pies as well. He was just a servant-hearted man like that.

He was funny too. One time he left me a gruff voicemail that went like this: "This is Joe."

I'm thinking, *Joe who? I don't recognize this person.*

After a pregnant pause in the voicemail, he said, "Joe daddy!" And then proceeded to crack up with laughter on the other end of the phone. That was my daddycakes. Never another one like him.

Another time before I drove away, he leaned into my Tahoe and hung a silver chain and pendant around my mirror, telling me it was for protection. I never really thought much about that necklace and pendant other than, *My daddy gave that to me, and he loves his baby girl.* I would hang my golf glove from that necklace after a great day at the range or on the course.

It wasn't until after he left this earth (in 2014), and his table and every other of his earthly belongings got transported to my house, that the picture got a little less fuzzy. One day on the way home from a fantastic day at the range and hot wings overlooking Nashville, I turned the corner to my house and the necklace caught a *Son*ray (you just wait . . . yes, I meant to type it this way) and almost blinded me. I grabbed the necklace at a stoplight and peered at the pendant, pulling it close to my face to study it. I almost caused a wreck at that intersection.

It read, *Saint Christopher*!

Immediately I began to bawl as I whispered to myself, "You did know, Papa, you did know! You knew it was him!" While my dad had never physically met my Christopher, it was as if he knew all along that he was coming down the road for me. It was the handoff that was supposed to happen at the end of the aisle at our wedding; it just happened in another space and time, another realm. And in some ways, it was even more significant because GOD knew he was never going to get to that point in our relationship and HE let my daddycakes hand me to him and him to me just a smidgen early.

To think that all these years on all these back roads, driving from sporting event to sporting event by myself while calling out to God to send me a husband or at the very least send me a sign, the sign was right there, mere inches from my face and etched on a piece of jewelry that was last touched by my precious papa.

His name: Christopher.

This one-upped the spice jars by a zillion. I pressed my hand so tight around that pendant when I got home that it almost pierced my skin.

I am a signs and wonders girl if you haven't figured that out by now. One of my favorite books is *When God Winks* by Squire Rushnell. It is full of miraculous stories of signs and wonders, but here's the deal: I really didn't *have* to read a book to see what was in front of me. I was and am living my signs-and-wonders life, full-tilt boogie, baby!

That same necklace now belongs to my husband. It hangs around his neck as a sign of my love and fidelity.

Before I knew, my daddycakes knew.

And that is everything to me.

My soul is smiling.

At our wedding, we exchanged wedding bands that belonged to my grandparents. In my hard, rocky, desolate places, I often wonder about that ring and the innermost parts of my grandparents' marriage, the parts many of us are too ashamed to show. Like Christopher, my grandfather had also been married before. What hurts did he bring into the marriage with my grandmother, and yet they endured? Every time I want to run back to old patterns, generational curses, or believe the lies of the enemy, I look at my husband's hand and that ring and it zaps me right in the heart.

We tend to show the pretty, the fancy, the expensive, the luxurious. I wonder what would happen if we began to show each other the parts of ourselves and our relationships we have desperately tried to keep hidden for so long. A revolution of healing, I bet. The act of trying to keep those things hidden is exhausting, you know?

Like it or not, whether married or single, platonic or non, work or personal, we all bring our hurts, scar tissue, and trauma with us into our relationships. The true challenge is learning to unpack the baggage together and then choosing not to carry it any further. Drop that suitcase off, my dear.

Drop it like it's hot!

Or, if you're like me, you might have to take one piece out at a time and attack it for a lifetime. (A gentle reminder here: everyone's healing journey looks different.) And there are times when I realize I've put a piece of baggage back in my suitcase, and I need to work on it, investigate it, analyze it, and sit with it. Pain has less power the more we sit with it.

My dad's table eventually went with me when I made the move to Yulee, Florida, to my new home with Christopher and my bonus kids. Immediately, it had kids and family and friends around it, laughing and experiencing joy, sweet joy. It had sticky places and stains like we all do, but that table was full-on loved and thoroughly used.

And even when I left, being the prodigal daughter that I was, the table remained. I wonder how many nights Christopher sat at it alone, elbows propping his head up as he rubbed his temples as he often does, pondering what would become of us. I know objects can't talk but much like the heavenly pendant handoff, I wonder if wisps of my father, who helped shape me, emanated up from that table and into an unsure Christopher. Maybe there were faint glimpses of hope or courage whispered to Christopher to go on when some around us were very on the fence about our future, given we had split twice now.

I think relationships, like people, cannot fit into a mold. No two are the same. And a lot aren't linear. They ebb, they flow, they break, they are put back together, and sometimes God puts us in *time-out*, separately, to heal.

That is the story of my Christopher and me. We are married and stronger today because of those breaks. We have a beautiful family because of those breaks. Don't you dare let the world or a person tell you that your relationship has to fit a cookie-cutter mold!

And while I was gone, in the physical sense, living two states over, he was surrounded by my things. He didn't have to look far to see pieces of me. He served breakfast and dinner and lunch to his kids, my future bonus kids, around that table. And while neither one of us knew what the future held for our relationship, apparently God and my daddycakes knew.

Recently, I watched my biological father, John, sit at my adoptive father's table and play cards with my bonus daughter for my birthday weekend and Memorial Day. I gripped the counter as I watched them quietly and intently. I felt love and gratitude burst from my chest for what God had done in my life and the life of my family. Have you ever felt love so palpably that you had to hold on to something for fear of falling over? It's a beautiful feeling. My dad in heaven never met my biological father, but I know he was grateful to him that he helped to create me and bring me into this world. Because of John, my biological father, my dad, David (daddycakes), got to be a father.

A quick aside: Because God is a God of overflow, the story continues. Not only was my biological dad sitting at this table, but also my stepdad, Gary, had spent many nights around this table with us, preparing our house for the upcoming wedding. Just like my biological dad was doing now, my stepdad had also integrated himself into the fabric of my new family. Sometimes I wonder what they might say if they all sat at that table together, my dads. What would they share? Would they get misty-eyed? I know beyond a doubt they would embrace each other, to the extent they could, all because of me. I was the tie that bound these men. Good gracious, God. You are the ultimate author, healer, and best weaver of stories. You are a good, good Father.

It was so much more than a card game I was watching, and it's so much more than a table. These people and that table are the manifestations of radical healing, forgiveness, the sacrificial love of adoption, the love of blended families, and generations of people who would have otherwise never known each other if there wasn't that love, sweet love. All these heirlooms—the necklace, the rings, the table—pointed to a story that was bigger than me. A story of healing that was generations in the making.

I catch myself a lot—when we have a full house around that table, with beautiful chaos swirling about—thinking about my dad sitting at the same table alone. While he never got the crowds and use that it sees now, how proud he must be at what has come of his table and more importantly his daughter. He got his wish; it just came in a different package and was delivered at a different time.

How often we think God has forgotten us when the package is on heaven's timeline, not ours. SHEWWW! If you want to get up and run around the block or give a fist bump to yourself after reading this, I'm totally okay with it; in fact, I encourage it!

What gifts, tangible or intangible, will you pass to the next generation? The benefactors might be your family, but they could also be total strangers. What will the "healed" you pass down that the "unhealed" you would have never been able to?

Your gifts, your talents, and most certainly your possessions will outlive you. And so will how you treated the people you leave behind, what you taught them, how you made them feel. What if we started thinking about legacy in terms of generational change and blessings? Blessings that touch people far beyond our life span, as when a multitude of generations were blessed through Abraham. You have that power within you, and it starts with a perspective change.

What you have and possess is not about you. It's greater than you and more far-reaching. And once you start to view your life and your time on this planet in that way, greed and selfishness start to fall away like scales on your eyes.

Your precious book collection—someone else will own that one day. Same goes for your coin collection. Maybe your kids have zero interest in inheriting it, but your neighbor boy, raised by a single mom working three jobs, does. He loves coins. What would that gift mean to him? The fact that you can speak three languages, have you passed them down or will they die with you? Who will get your dining room table? Your other possessions?

And here's a big one: Can you envision your babies or grandbabies being blessed in the way you wanted for yourself? Can you imagine a total stranger, one you may never meet, being blessed because you adopted this mindset and changed your perspective?

Even if it never happens for you, can you find joy in imagining the work you do within yourself blessing future generations? That's true relentless joy, being happy even when it doesn't directly affect you. I want you to cultivate pure joy especially when it happens to other people.

I remember donating items after a natural disaster. I thumbed through my things, deciding what to give. There was my worn stuff, my used stuff, but there was also a like-new, used-one-time tent and a gorgeous white dress someone could surely use after losing every worldly possession. After some inner deliberation, God won, not my flesh, and I happily donated more than a few brand-new items. I will never know who went camping in that tent, but I believe a family roasted s'mores and reconnected under the stars while using it. And I will never ever know this side of heaven who wore that dress, but I like to think it was worn proudly by someone walking across a stage with a diploma in hand, ready to take on the world!

Even if it never happens for you, can you find joy in imagining the work you do within yourself blessing future generations?

I don't share this to pat myself on the back; I was hesitant to give away my new and unused things. But when I did, oh, the relentless joy I experienced. It was as if the blessing my stuff was going to offer another—one that I would never fully know—boomeranged back onto me.

My father's table, his spice jars, and his giving me the name of my husband long before I ever knew him woke me up to legacy living, but being there to witness my mama dying cemented everything. After seeing her depart this earth, I am keenly aware of my own mortality. Watching someone I love leave this planet and realizing that our earthly bodies are just a shell got my attention really quickly. In an instant, she was gone; her life force, her energy, and her time in this life had ceased. But what I know to be true is that she was immediately with Jesus: "Today you will be with me in paradise" (Luke 23:43).

We are not long on this planet, my love. I want to awaken you to living out loud in such a way that your legacy lives on in the lives of others.

JOYSTART

Look at your life—your gifts, your talents, your physical possessions—in totality, in a much larger and longer sense. Make a list of your worldly possessions and your talents. Think long and hard. Maybe you have to keep coming back to the list for an extended period of time. Now think about how each of these things could live on beyond you. Write down your wishes for each thing. (And let it be known to others, so people don't go squabbling after you, too, leave this planet.) Be specific and proactive.

Now sit for a moment, still and quiet, and put your hand over your heart and soul. Feel your heartbeat and imagine all that you are and all you have spreading out into the world like a ripple on a pond to bless others. Journal about what might come of the healing work God wants to do in your heart. How will your hard work today impact kids, grandkids, and anyone else you encounter? Consider this and thank God for what he will do in the future. Bask in the pure and true joy for just a moment. Now open your eyes, joystarter.

I love you.

I see you trying.

Your soul is beautiful.

I'm proud of you.

CHAPTER 12

In His Time

I have always heard the adage, "It will happen when you least expect it." If I had a dollar for every time that was spoken to me, I might have amassed a fortune. Literally. I was really tired of the platitude. My soul was weary. Dating as a Christian woman is exhausting. Heck, dating is exhausting, period. On one Bumble date in Nashville, the suitor and I sipped coffees and exchanged pleasantries about our churches.

He abruptly asked me, "How do you do it? It must be so tough."

"Do what?" I responded.

"Date when there are so many beautiful women in Nashville that you are competing against."

Now fam, I'm not going to lie to you, I almost spit my piping-hot Starbucks on Romeo's face, but I was able to gather all my dignity and belief in myself and respond calmly.

"Honey, I don't compete," I said. "I am who I am. I love myself, and I'm not in competition with anyone but myself." Suffice to say, that was the last time I ever saw this dude.

And here's an altogether different story. I was messaging with a potential suitor, and after a week or so, he told me he was getting back together with an ex but asked if it was okay if he called me if things did not work out. Fam! My head jerked back so quickly upon reading his message that I almost gave myself whiplash while sitting still in a recliner.

This was my plight. It was bleak, and I was weary. I remember getting to a point—from the fetal position, mind you—where I uttered to God, "You are enough. If marriage and motherhood aren't in the cards for me, You are enough."

If you are single or have a single friend or family member—that should cover all of us—I encourage you to call and read this chapter to them, aloud. Buy them this book!

Numerous things helped me while dating. I want to share those with you and/or the single people in your life. And for those of you not dating—or who have found the person you will date for the rest of your life—don't tune out! Even though there is a lot about dating in this chapter, you can still learn a ton about waiting. Waiting well is a big part of living with relentless joy. Waiting for the right job, friendships, church, or other life situation.

Okay, that being said, let's have some real talk!

First, having clear standards is essential. Hon, your joy is dependent on you having standards, or nonnegotiables as I like to call them.

Here were a few of mine for dating:

- He must be a believer. Of Jesus. Being spiritual didn't work for me. I did quite enough missionary dating in my life. I needed someone who already loved the Lord and knew Him personally.
- He must love his family and be open to loving mine. I can't handle a guy who is going to be rude to his mama!
- He must love kids. 'Nough said.

- He must be willing to wait for marriage to be physically intimate as a way of honoring God and ourselves. (I know, radical. But I'm a radical girl for Jesus.)

This is a small sample of what I hoped and desired in a partner, but they were things I was not willing to budge on.

And let me speak to the fellas here. You should absolutely make a list too! I don't know what is most important to you but here are some points I imagine might make your heart happy!

- She is strong, kind, and passionate.
- She is driven about her dreams.
- She is selfless and prioritizes others.
- She challenges me and makes me better.
- I can take her home to my mama, and my mama loves her. (Or my mama would've loved her.)
- Dad feels the same.
- She's comfortable around my people and makes a big effort with my family and friends, especially my kids (if applicable), or any kids for that matter.
- We have the same belief system.
- She's motivated.
- She takes care of herself.

Is any of this resonating? (I'm grinning so big as I type it!)

Get a piece of paper (or just use the margins) and write down your nonnegotiables for dating or another form of waiting—for example, for your next job, your friendships, your faith community, and so on. What are you not willing to budge on? It's important to know these things and be able to communicate them.

And for goodness' sake, let's make our standards more than skin-deep. I often teach people this: looks will fade, so please make sure you are curious about your potential mate. There will be days when you want to claw each other's eyeballs out, but the deeper connection, curiosity, and commitment will keep you coming back together for a lifetime.

I also found it really important to constantly evaluate myself—albeit really uncomfortable. I asked myself often, "Would you want to date you?" And then I would sit with the answer. If the answer made me uncomfortable, I would work to grow in that area. I want you to do the same. You have that power. I often find people wanting a "good" guy or girl when they themselves don't constitute their own definition of good.

While teaching from many stages, I have shared this simple truth: like attracts like. So while you may be able to attract a queen or king or royal, you will not keep them if you are not on that same level.

I'm gonna ask you an uncomfortable question: Are you joyful to be around, or are you a drag? Would you want to be married to you?

I know these might be tough questions to ask yourself, but I think they are vital. So much of who we are in our relationships with others starts within us. Before I met Christopher, I stopped trying to *find the one* and focused on *being the one*. Woo-wee! That just gave me goose bumps as I typed.

If I don't like me, how can I expect anyone else to? The same goes for loving yourself. I think you put off a crazy shine and magnetism when you truly love yourself. And loving yourself isn't all roses, just like loving another person isn't. Instead, I would offer this: I love myself so much because God created me. (Duh, and He doesn't make mistakes.) But also, I love myself so much that I know the spots I need to work on. And if I'm blind to them, I am open and willing for my loved ones to point out those rough edges because they truly have my best interest at heart.

When is the last time you giggled uncontrollably? When is the last time you danced or skipped or painted or journaled? When is the last time you did something to better yourself? All these things make you a happier, more joyful human being.

In your mind, go on a date with yourself. I know, seems silly, but follow me here. Are you engaging or do you talk all about yourself? BORING! Do you ask questions? Are you curious about the person across from you? Do you gossip about people and spread negativity? (I've been guilty of this. No judgment here.) Or do you talk about ideas, travel, books, magical circumstances, and miracles?

If you don't like the date sitting across from you (which is yourself), then change it. Change you! Change you, baby! It's not too late. Sidenote: when I say "change you," I don't mean pretend to be a different person. I mean change to be the best you possible!

Let me remind you of a beautiful truth: you are not defective; you are under construction, my dear (like we all are). Anytime we are trying, learning, seeking, pushing, and working to be better versions of ourselves, we are under construction. There is zero shame in that. I will be working on myself until the day that I depart this earth. I am a proud queen under construction!

I want it to be the same for you! If you will put these truths into practice, I promise you more laughter, more joy, more peace, more promise, more hope, more blessed assurance that you are a miracle by God's hand. You just need your hard hat and shovel. If you want to keep from becoming stale, angry, and bitter, your hat and shovel are as necessary as the air you breathe.

Another thing I realized as I dated is that I needed to be secure with myself on my own if I was going to be truly secure with myself while with someone else. I am a words-of-affirmation person; it's one of my love languages.[1] Huge shoutout to Gary Chapman for such valuable insight on how we all tick. I also love that his work can be used for kids, other family, coworkers, and more. But here's the thing: I have to affirm myself first. I have to love myself in such a way that I am not dependent on anyone else to complete me. And if today, you are having a hard time loving and affirming yourself, let me help you out with a few biblical affirmations:

I am a chosen generation and a royal priesthood, holy and special (see 1 Pet. 2:9).

God has plans for me to prosper and have hope for the future (see Jer. 29:11).

God is my safe place; I go to Him because I trust Him (see Ps. 91:2).

The Lord will provide me with the desires of my heart (see Ps. 37:4).

My mourning will be turned into dancing (see Ps. 30:11).

My sorrows will be turned into joy (see John 16:20).

As I wait on God, my power is renewed (see Isa. 40:31).

The Lord will cause blessings to overtake me (see Deut. 28:2).

My children will be blessed (see Deut. 28:4).

These things are true of you even if you struggle to believe them. Unless we arm ourselves with what God says about us—what the B-I-B-L-E says about us—we are so susceptible to what the world and the broken people in it say about us.

I should know. There were periods in my waiting when I let the devil invade my thoughts and win the temporary battle of my mind. (Hello, Joyce Meyer!) My childhood wounds (that he also inflamed) came raging back.

I wasn't enough. I was too much. I wasn't lovable. There was something wrong with me. I needed to be less me. My standards were impossible. I was going to be alone forever. These thoughts plagued me when I got up and when I laid my head down to rest; they popped up during the day. And these: I didn't have a snatched waist. My body wasn't toned enough. I was too emotional. I didn't have a six-pack. I was too much altogether, and that is why I wasn't in a flourishing relationship.

What a crock of bull.

None of it was true, but I bought it, hook, line, and sinker, and it was making me sick. I knew I was precious, I knew I was unique and valuable and set apart, but I let the world and it's toxicity tell me otherwise. Anyone feel me?

Until I finally started to realize what God was whispering to me all along: "You are enough!"

I wrapped my soul in this truth like a bulletproof vest. I sat with it, reminded myself of it, embraced it as a mantra. From that moment forward, there were still negative thoughts. (I wouldn't lie to you because what good would that do either of us?) But they weren't as persistent, and they would flee because I now had on the armor of God—the armor of His truth.

Recently, I taught my bonus baby, Leah, how to arm herself with His armor. Let me give you a refresher from the living Word:

> Put on the full armor of God, so that you can take your stand against the devil's schemes. For our struggle is not against flesh and blood, but against the rulers, against the authorities, against the powers of this dark world and against the spiritual forces of evil in the heavenly realms. Therefore put on the full armor of God, so that when the day of evil comes, you may be able to stand your ground, and after you have done everything, to stand. Stand firm then, with the belt of truth buckled around your waist, with the breastplate of righteousness in place, and with your feet fitted with the readiness that comes from the gospel of peace. In addition to all this, take up the shield of faith, with which you can extinguish all the flaming arrows of the evil one. Take the helmet of salvation and the sword of the Spirit, which is the word of God. (Eph. 6:11–17)

The world will throw flaming arrows at you, my friend. We must learn to be on the offensive.

I've often heard pastors say that we will go crazy at a football game or a concert, yet we are meek or hesitant to go crazy when it comes to our faith. I say, let's go crazy! Go crazy for your marriages.

Go crazy for your babies' marriages and your friends' marriages. Go crazy for your kids and their love lives. And if you're not married, go crazy about your future marriage or your future kids or your future calling or maybe even just your future self.

Call it out!

Put on your war paint, baby! Grab your shield and let's get ready because we are in a battle every single day!

In the fall of 2017, I boarded a plane bound for Montgomery, Alabama. I was the lone female speaker in Montgomery Quarterback Club's season series of speakers. My mom drove over from Georgia along with her lifelong bestie Sandra to surprise me. (Surprising one another every chance we got was my mama's and my unique love language.) The three of us arrived at the venue that evening where I was set to speak, and I was ushered to a separate room for pics with people and media interviews. (This still makes me giggle, by the way; the fact that someone wants my autograph is beyond me.)

Sidenote: may your success never go to your head, my love. My mom used to say, "Don't get too big for your britches." It's a classic Southern saying meaning enjoy it, but don't get a big head.

So here I am, taking pics with people, and in walks this stunning man. I must admit, I am a sucker for a man in a suit, and boy was this man *wearing* his suit, if you know what I mean! It hugged every place it was designed to!

SHEW! Is it hot in here? Good thing he was a tall drink of water.

When he stepped up to take a picture, I noticed his beautiful, huge hands and chiseled jawline. He smelled good too! We exchanged pleasantries and for the first time since that summer, something stirred deep inside of me. I had been ghosted (when someone cuts off all communication without explanation) the past summer by someone I really liked, and I was still shook, still hurt, still sad. But this handsome stranger made me curious in a way I hadn't been since being slighted a few months back.

He departed for his seat, and I continued to take pictures with the rest of the people in line. The event was starting soon, so I gathered myself to get ready to speak and entered the ballroom, searching for my mom and her bestie in the crowd. I quickly scanned the room, and to my utter shock and amazement, the handsome stranger was sitting next to my mother, chatting away!

What?

I sat down to his left; my mother was at his right. They continued to chat, my mother gazing adoringly at him. He was showing her pictures of his kids and speaking of them glowingly.

He must be married, I thought disappointedly. *He's just not wearing a ring.*

The slight hope I had let myself feel earlier quickly dissipated. I was moments away from taking the stage and needed to focus anyhow. As I spoke, I avoided looking at my table. Sometimes it's just easier that way—not to look at those I love when I'm speaking. Plus, the handsome stranger was sitting there. Once I was done and the event was wrapping up, the handsome stranger bought one of everything from my swag table in the back. (My mother, aka my mom-ager, had graciously brought things with her to sell on my behalf. Ever the saleswoman, with her true charm and sweet soul, she could sell ice to an Eskimo.)

We all took a few more pics and then the man, who I had learned was named Christopher, turned to me and said, "What's your number so I can text you these pictures?" In an instant, I knew he wasn't taken and that this was his way of getting connected. He was smooth, really smooth.

Later that night, we were back at our hotel. It was customary for the speaker to go downstairs to the adjoining restaurant to mingle with the people who had attended the event. I had learned that Christopher just happened to be staying at the same hotel. Of all the hotels in the city, he was at ours! My mom and I made our way to the restaurant. I saw a long table of ten or so people but no Christopher. Since I had his number, I texted to ask if he was coming downstairs. He joined us a bit later but was seated at the other end of the table. Between us sat several type A people who had a lot to say. A lot! I stole glances at the other end of the table to survey this man: blond, confident, good with people, and easy on the eyes.

My hope was back, and this time it was doing the Samba in my belly.

The crowd started to dissipate, and my mom went upstairs to the room I was sharing with her and her friend. It was just Christopher and me for the first time since meeting each other. We sat down in the oversized chairs in the lobby to finally chat one-on-one. He leaned forward, elbows on his long, long legs, and said possibly the most valiant words I've ever heard: "I'm interested in dating you."

I was aghast . . . in the best possible way. The little girl in me recognized a knight that was declaring his intentions. His words made every fairy tale come true in my heart. He wanted me but not in a let-me-take-you-upstairs way. He wanted to get to know me, to court me.

And this is an important truth in a world that is hypersexualized. I want you to be wanted, wanted for life. I also want you to be wanted for your heart and soul. I want you to be wanted for how you light up a room with your humor or your laughter. I want you to be wanted for all the things besides your looks or sex appeal.

I want you to be wanted, not lusted after.

And there is a huge difference. You are worth the wait, my love. (I'm talking to you too, men!) And I don't care what you've done or where you've been. You are never too far gone to begin again. Let God draw a line in the sand and redeem you and make you anew. Don't fall for that trick of the enemy. He wants to keep you silent and shamed.

I get to share my testimony at the Lovelady Center in Birmingham, Alabama, twice a year. I have been going and sharing for almost ten years. Envision hundreds of hungry women, some fresh out of jail, many with their children, gathered together at this Christian halfway house. I lovingly like to call it a "whole-way house," because they give the women the opportunity to bring their kids to stay with them, offer a school where the women can get an education and job training, provide medical and dental assistance, and most importantly, they give them Jesus.

When I share, the women hang off the four levels of balconies overlooking the worship space, many battling addictions and/or recovering from years of prostitution. They hoot, they holler, they affirm, they sing out, they dance, they cry, with hands—and sometimes babies—raised in the air. I've been incredibly blessed to attend the best concerts and events all over this beautiful planet, and still, nothing has ever compared energy-wise to the palpable and buzzing current *Don't fall for* in that room. The air is electric with hope each *that trick of* and every time. It is the energy of healing, of truth, *the enemy. He* of the Waymaker on the move; it's the energy of *wants to keep* the Good Shepherd coming back for the one lost sheep. *you silent*

And here's a truth that deserves repeating: we *and shamed.* have all been that lost sheep at one time or another in our lives.

Over the years and countless visits, I have held these women in my arms and told them, without a shadow of a doubt, that Jesus can make them anew, that He can wash them white as snow. One of my greatest joys is sharing this irrefutable truth with them. If they proclaim the name of Jesus, whether they've been violated or sold their body for drugs, they are a new creature in Christ.

These experiences at the Lovelady and all the waiting I had done made Christopher's words that night ("I'm interested in dating you") that much more meaningful and honorable. I wanted to cry right there, but thank goodness I didn't. Instead, I stammered out, "Ah . . . okay!"

He walked me upstairs and gave me a kiss on the cheek before departing for his own room. All the while this was happening, my mother was texting me like a madwoman.

"Where are you? I am worried!"

Keep in mind it was before midnight, and we never left the hotel. Just goes to show you that you are never too old to be your mama's baby. From that day forward, there was never another day that Christopher William Rohe would not be in my heart. We instantly became best friends, confidants, and smitten as two kittens. I met his children and fell further in love with him and them.

We discovered what we had in common—mainly that we are both history nerds. The neatest thing Christopher and I do is send articles and history facts and anecdotes back and forth. Our first stop, hands down, in a new area is a museum. We also learned to appreciate the other person. If I golf, he drives the cart. If he drives the car, I have learned to put my phone down, be present, and have conversations with him. (He drives a lot; sorry, Christopher.) We laughed and talked and became fascinated with each other. We learned to appreciate the little things. Isn't that what's important in every relationship from work to home?

We grew, we fought, we grew some more. And even when we weren't together as a couple, we were never really apart because sometimes a breakup isn't really a breakup. Sometimes it's God's way of saying, "In my time. I need to do some healing."

JOYSTART

Are you ready to go on a date . . . with yourself? Yes, YOU! Have you ever dined as one? Gone to a movie by yourself? Planned a solo picnic? Gone on a solo bike ride or hike (take personal protection, people!)? I want you to do it because until you are happy on your own, you won't ever be truly joyful with another human being. To give good love to others, you have to truly love yourself first! And what if you took this book and/or your journal along and you made notes on who you want to be and who you want to attract (if you're single and looking to date)? Take time to see that play out in your head. Envision you loving you! And envision you in a happy, committed relationship too. I know it may be terrifying to take these

154

steps, but remember, beloved, the magic happens in the uncomfortable and unknown space.

You got this.

You're brave.

You can do this.

I love you!

CHAPTER 13

Miracles in Disguise

I got cozy in my seat on the airplane, quickly buckling my seat belt before letting out a huge sigh. I LOVE what I do, but sometimes getting there and home can be taxing, as I'm sure anyone who travels for a living would tell you. But I do love the airport. This might sound unbelievable to some, along with the dreaded gate changes and mad dashes while covered in sweat, but there are sweet hellos, precious goodbyes, and oh, the genuine emotions!

I love seeing soldiers and first responders and thanking them for their service. I love being crazy kind to people, and when I am not, I love trying to make up for it by either apologizing to that person or trying to be extra kind to the next person I encounter on my journey.

If you ever encounter me in an airport alone, you'll see I'm almost always talking to myself or reassuring myself that I am indeed going to make it. (And am I the only one who just needs to see their gate, with their own two eyes, before proceeding to the bathroom or grabbing food?) Traveling, particularly by air, is a whole journey unto itself.

To my left on this particular flight was a man dressed in de-signer duds. He was really well put together, to put it quite sim-ply. We got to talking about life while we were on our flight. I'm quick to go deep; I rarely talk about surface level stuff and when I do, it is not for long. He told me he was a photographer in LA and proceeded to show me a gaggle of beautiful people he had photographed at fancy Hollywood parties. I was impressed and I told him so. He had a real eye for photography. His work seemed to take an already aesthetically pleasing person and make them jump off the screen by highlighting one of their features. It was really magical.

I know I use that word a lot, but I experience magic daily. It is all around us and within us. I am magical—most days—and you are magical, my friend.

He went on to tell me he was self-taught.

I slapped him on the arm and said, "No way! Wow, you are *really* talented!"

He told me he had been in a motorcycle accident and was flat on his back recovering for an extended period of time. He thought, *Well, I should teach myself something while I'm lying here,* so he got on YouTube and taught himself the art of photography. Now look, I'm impressed daily by people, what they've been through, how they've coped and survived and persevered, but I was blown away by this young man.

He told me about the first big party he went to photograph as a gig. He stood outside nervously with sweaty palms. The nasty, doubting voice in his head, which I now know to be the devil or one of his demons, told him to turn around, that he was a fraud and a failure. But he didn't turn around, he didn't move. Instead, he began to cheer for himself, he began to reassure himself, and when he moved, he moved his butt inside that building to do the dang thing! This is how he ended up sitting next to me on this flight, on his way to his next big photography gig, because he nailed the gig he almost ran from.

I looked over at him and exclaimed, probably a tad too excitedly for my surroundings, "YOU ARE LIKE THE BLACK FRIDA KAHLO!"

He looked puzzled. "Who?"

A giddiness washed over me, and all my Latina cells stood at attention. This was my chance to brag about *mi cultura*. (Not only were my cells standing, but they were also doing the Samba under my skin. I was that excited.) I proceeded to tell him about a young woman named Frida Kahlo who, one day in 1925, was riding a bus in Mexico City. No sooner had she taken her seat on the bus when it turned the corner and collided with an electric trolley car. She was impaled by a metal rod and suffered many broken bones. Several passengers were killed instantly, and several later died from their injuries.

Kahlo's pelvic bone was fractured, and the impalement had punctured her abdomen and uterus. Her spine was broken in three places, her right leg in eleven places; her shoulder was dislocated, and her collar bone was broken. Doctors would later find three more vertebrae broken. She was a mess medically speaking. She endured many surgeries (in her lifetime, she had thirty surgeries), and then for many months was on bed rest, bound up in a body cast. While she had originally wanted to go to medical school, the accident forced her to drop out. Her father, an accomplished German photographer, had always encouraged her artistic side, so when she was bedridden for so long, a special lap easel was set up for her and she began to paint even more, oftentimes using a mirror and herself as the subject of the painting.[1]

She would go on to be one of the most iconic female painters of all time. Many of her paintings depict the struggles she went through in her life, beginning before the accident as she suffered from polio and had a limp. She would go on to fall in love with a charismatic muralist named Diego Rivera. The two were fiery lovers who divorced and later remarried, but their marriage was always dogged by infidelity from both sides. Frida desperately wanted a child, but complications from the accident left her scarred. She had multiple miscarriages and struggled with infertility for the rest of her life.

Her pain and joy and heritage were front and center in her paintings. She painted about it all. Just like I talk about all the parts of life, she painted about hers. And the result was tragically marvelous. Her paintings didn't shy away from the shadows in her life; rather, she embraced them and brought her pain out onto full display. There on those canvases were the best of her and the worst of her.

Frida was certainly well-known during her lifetime, and she traveled the globe for her exhibitions as a result of her fame. But it's safe to say that her legacy grew steadily posthumously since the '70s. And today, many would say we are Frida-crazy, as you can find every sort of swag with her paintings or famous unibrow across it. She is thought by some to be one of the most well-known artists of the twentieth century. While there is much more to her story that I hope you check out, the huge takeaway here is that her horrific accident and subsequent surgeries and complications, however painful, were actually the gateway to her enormous talent, to her gift.

After explaining all this, my new friend on the airplane was astonished. He finally got the comparison, and I could tell he felt the weight of it as I watched that knowledge slowly creep across his face. It was a palpable feeling that we shared right there on that airplane. His astonishment and gratitude were so real that it felt like you could slice the air between us with a knife.

Both of these human beings—Frida and my photographer friend—used an accident to become talented artists.

Many, including me at times in my life, would have swum in the baby pool of self-pity, acting all "Woe is me!" But not these two. They turned their pain into a beautiful talent that would in turn bless so many others.

I can't tell you when I first fell in love with Frida, but all who know me, even marginally well, know she's my spirit animal. There isn't a week that goes by when someone doesn't send me a picture of a reproduction painting of hers, a purse with her face emblazoned upon it, or a shirt from a store that is honoring her in some way. I have seen her painted on the side of restaurants and on the walls inside. I'm always like, "Hey girl. It's been a while!" And I give her a cosmic high five and hug!

I have been to her blue house in Mexico that is now a museum. I have seen her art at the Museo de Arte Moderno/Museum of Modern Art. I have seen her paintings on tour in Atlanta and Nashville, and soon I will see her special immersive installation. I don't know how to describe my pull to her other than to say I feel a deep connection to her. I always have, even before I knew who she was. And when I did discover her, it was like meeting a long-lost friend. Maybe it is our Mexican-ness or our spunk or our refusal to lay down and die, but I have always been deeply attracted to her grit and her guts.

I'm simply gobsmacked by people who turn something searingly painful into something so beautiful.

Sidenote: while writing this particular chapter, I gave myself a literal hug. It hit me that the reason I identify so strongly with Frida and the relative stranger on the plane is because I am one of them. I am someone who has turned my mess into my message. I'm not a photographer or a painter, but I am an artist in my own way. They used paintbrushes and a camera; the tool I use is my voice. (I wonder what tools you have in your arsenal?)

Have you been flat on your back in life, down on your luck? Broke, addicted, broken, depressed, hurt?

I have too. It's time to dust yourself off and make something beautiful from all that pain. No guts, no glory, my people. It's time to go big or go home! And the most comforting part of this advice? You don't have to do it alone. Consider this verse:

> To all who mourn in Israel,
>   he will give a crown of beauty for ashes,
> a joyous blessing instead of mourning,
>   festive praise instead of despair.

In their righteousness, they will be like great oaks
that the LORD has planted for his own glory.
(Isa. 61:3 NLT)

I don't pretend to know if Frida was a believer (although it would
be amazing to see her in heaven), but I do remember turning to
my friend on the airplane and telling him, "You know you are a
miracle, right?"

He sheepishly agreed.

We talked about the great work that was done in his life by God
Almighty. He very well could've died on that bike, but he didn't.
He is alive for all to see. He is alive for fortuitous individuals like
myself to experience his life force, his good, his talent. He is alive
to be a witness that God is still very much in the miracle-making
business.

And guess what? YOU ARE A MIRACLE TOO! Your story isn't
over yet, not by a country mile. And let me tell you about a country
mile. They are long, and oftentimes you get lost and have to begin
again. Sometimes you miss the turn at the red mailbox across from
farmer John's field. You have to start over and retrace your steps, a
lot like life if you think about it.

In my own life, retracing my steps has resulted in me being able
to say that being dragged through the house by my hair led me to
travel coast to coast, speaking to men about never letting that happen in their presence and being men who would never lay a hand
on a woman.

I also know for a fact that having suicidal ideations and being *this*
close to using the gun on the top of my refrigerator to take my life
actually hid within it *a blueprint (full of relentless joy) to save millions
of other lives.* What the devil meant to take me out was the catalyst
to save so many others!

It reminds me of one of my favorite verses: "And we know that in
all things God works for the good of those who love him, who have
been called according to his purpose" (Rom. 8:28).

Let's break down this Scripture together, my peeps. *All things*, that doesn't just mean the good things, the happy things, the pretty things, the things you want to show to others. The apostle Paul truly means ALL things: the ugly, the scarred, the dead, the broken, the bitter, ALL THINGS! God takes ALL these things and He works them out for our good, for those who are called according to His purpose.

Which is all of us. Even if you've strayed, backslidden, been church-hurt or people-hurt or never known Him before, He still has a plan for your life. And He is calling you according to His purpose. He has a beautiful plan to turn all the things you have experienced into something so ever-loving beautiful!

That'll preach.

What was meant to destroy me didn't. The same goes for Frida and my friend on the airplane. The same goes for you.

As I was writing this chapter I stumbled upon this quote:

> People speak of hope as if it's this delicate, ephemeral thing made of whispers and spider's webs. It's not. Hope has dirt on her face, blood on her knuckles, the grit of cobblestones in her hair, and just spat out a tooth as she rises for another go.[2]

I dig this; I feel it deeply. I am hope. You are hope. We are fighters. We have cobblestones in our hair, and we just spat out a tooth. Well, scratch that last part. We can do without losing any teeth, but you get the point! We will overcome and make something beautiful from our ashes. And God will be there guiding us and cheering us on the entire way.

Hope while you wait expectantly. There is joy in hope, and there is joy in the waiting.

And if there is no beauty yet, then hope fiercely for the beauty that is coming down the road, my warrior friend! Hope while you wait expectantly. There is joy in hope, and there is joy in the waiting. I am living proof of this.

What skill have you always wanted to learn? It's there for the taking. I tell people all the time that YouTube is a heck of a teacher. (I think I've even mentioned it once already in this book.) You can learn literally anything on that website. If you don't have time, start getting up fifteen minutes earlier. After you've done that for thirty days, make it thirty minutes. Master that for another thirty days and make it forty-five minutes. I know people who have added so much value to their day by making time for something. Don't die wishing you had always learned to play the piano. Learn to tickle those dang ivories! Life is short and it is precious, and none of us know how long we have. I am begging you to start making the most of your days.

I once saw a meme on the internet that depicted a long line of people. At the beginning of the line, people seemed to be heading up in the sky somewhere, one by one. The caption read, "We are all walking each other home." This image and these words have stuck with me forever.

I am walking you home.

You are walking me home.

And we have no idea where we are in that line. You could be at the tail end and have many more days, but you could also be close to the front, my dear.

Learn to play the piano. (Or whatever it is your heart is yearning to do.)

Start seeing your failures as miracles in disguise.

Choose better.

Talk to the person on the plane sitting next to you.

Because you haven't even met all the people that are going to love you (and vice versa)! That's wildly beautiful! Bring it on!

We just don't know about any of it: our days, who we are about to meet, how our needs are going to be met, the miracles we are about to experience, the valleys we are going to go through.

So hold on, my love.

Hold on to your joy.

On the airplane that day, I took a moment to feel my own skin, my own bones, my own mortality, my own life force. I felt the sacredness of my days, however many I may have left. I thanked myself—and more importantly thanked GOD—for turning so many ugly things in my life into something extraordinarily radiant. Yes, I am one of these people, and I want to give you an invitation to the other side of your ugly.

JOYSTART

I would love for you to write down all the accidents, the screwups, and what you deem as failures in your life. Yep, write them down. Then retrace them. Study them. Look them in the eye. Now look at your list again. I double-dog dare you to write the beauty that has come from any of the horrific things you wrote down. If you cannot find the beauty, ask God how He wants to bring redemption from that pain.

CHAPTER 14

It Starts with a YES!

I was adopted at eighteen months old by my daddycakes. I've been open in this book about how beautiful I think adoption is. It's the act of saying, I want you. You are loved. I give you my name. I give you my life. It's the act of saying "YES!" to another vulnerable and needy soul. I don't know about you, but being wanted matters a great deal to me.

As I've mentioned, I joke with people and tell them if I had a sitcom, it would be called *My Three Dads*. I have a stepdad, a biological dad, and an adoptive dad. I even have a bonus dad, my brothers' father. We have the same mom but different dads. And because my brothers are older, my bonus dad, Daddy Bryan, has known me since birth and always loved me. So maybe it is really *My Four Dads*!

While my life hasn't been perfect in terms of my father story, the fact that I was adopted makes me feel very much wanted and very much loved. Not to mention the relationship I have with my biological father today and my stepfather and my bonus dad.

But let's talk adoption. I've always had the heart for it, but not everyone is cut out to adopt and that is okay. It really does take a unique heart. Before I met Christopher, I was taking classes to adopt a sibling group. I remember being in the room with other prospective parents, the parents being couples, and there was singular me, little old me in Franklin, Tennessee, at a church for PATH (Parents as Tender Healers) classes. I was shaking like a leaf but wholly resolute in being there. It was a calling, a longing in my soul. So many people thought I was insane, and they tried to talk me out of it. But those closest to me knew I was as serious as the day is long. They also knew I couldn't be dissuaded. I knew I had the capacity and the heart to love a sibling group.

While the other prospective parents were after a baby, I wanted to keep a set of kids together, even if they were older. I had heard every horror story to try to talk me out of adopting: an adopted child knifing a mattress to smithereens, another attacking a biologically born child, another having to be sent back to God knows where. I had to get real in terms of my support community and how it all would work when I traveled for work, which was often. These were all things I was pondering and planning but ultimately trusting God to work out.

Then I met Christopher, and his four beautiful children walked into my life. They stole my heart, hook, line, and sinker. I was a goner. And while they have a wonderful mother and obviously an amazing father, they still gave me space in their hearts to allow me to love them as well. This incredible blessing has put my plans to adopt on the back burner for now, but my heart to see people wanted and chosen has not changed.

A couple of years back when I first started #ImChangingthe Narrative, somebody very wise said to me, "You don't get it, do you?"

"Get what?" I asked.

"I know your heart for adoption, and while it hasn't happened in a traditional sense, it really has. Because look at all these players and kids across the country that look at you like a mother figure. You fill a need, and in that way you've adopted hundreds of times over."

Needless to say, I bawled big, grateful, salty tears.

I marinated on that for a long time, and I still do to this day. I don't take these relationships I am blessed to forge and grow lightly.

Many people in the speaking profession get on planes, fly someplace, speak, pick up their checks, and leave. And while there's absolutely nothing wrong with that, zero, it's not how I operate. It's not how I'm built. I stay no matter how long it takes. We hug and cry afterward. Some of my audience waits until everyone leaves to unload their story and pent-up emotions. Others send lengthy messages or call me.

Even during the pandemic, I gave out my phone number. People thought I was absolutely insane, but no one has ever abused it. I just didn't want people in crisis to have to go through social media to get ahold of me while we were all hurting so badly. There were some players I've worked with over the years, three to be exact, who reached out in their time of crisis. We were able to get them help. They are now thriving and living their best lives.

I can't simply speak and leave. I crave human connection. I live to see the light go on in someone's soul. I long for them to know that they are chosen, that they are wanted. It is how I'm built. It is who I am. I am all about the long-term lens.

I tell those I speak to: "For some of you, you will walk out of here and never be the same. A lot of you are skeptical, but if you will open your heart a millimeter to what I have to share, I promise you will walk out of here and NEVER BE THE SAME! How do I know? Because I've spoken to thousands, and they have reported back about their life change. Whether that be forgiving a family member, forgiving themselves, asking for help, not struggling alone, setting boundaries, or learning to radically love themselves, there is real life change waiting within my story if you will open your heart. For some of you, I will attend your wedding; for some, I will see pictures from the delivery room when your baby is born. I want to be in your life. I want to be in your life for the long haul, and I want to fill whatever role you need to be filled. And for others, what I share today/tonight will be enough. You will remember something I said for the rest of your life."

Then there are others who sleep through my talks. I don't usually mention that, but I figured I'd say it here. I have learned not to take it personally. Maybe they wrestled with anxiety the night before and didn't get any sleep. Maybe they are achingly homesick and too ashamed to talk about it. Maybe they stayed out and partied the night before, or maybe it was just the rigors of athletics or work or school, and everything else that comes with those things. I came for one, and if there are more than that, great! I have run my race for that specific day and done my job well.

My friend Justin Batt, founder of Daddy Saturday—a movement designed to encourage dads and end fatherlessness—has shared that he will often ask God, "Lord, what do you have for me today? What message? What lesson? Who am I supposed to touch?"

I just love this. He has taught me to take an active approach in asking God to reveal to me what He needs me to do on His behalf that given day or what He wants me to learn.

Radical stuff, man. I dig it.

Because make no mistake, you have heavenly assignments. I have heavenly assignments. In my own life, there is no other way to look at what I do. The staggering amount of life change I've seen because of this movement and the work we do, the people who have chosen to serve their guts out beside me for peanuts or no pay at all, the weekly messages I get that never make it to the public eye, and the level of spiritual warfare I battle in the most sacred places of my life. All of these confirm to me that I am running the race that Yahweh intended for me.

Instead of waiting until the end of this chapter, I'm going to ask you a few joystart questions now just to get your juices flowing early. What do you think your heavenly assignment might be? If heaven gave you a job title, what would it be? Where does your heart break when you look at the world around you? Where does a need collide with your passion and gifting? How might you start using that passion and gifting to work toward making a difference in that space even today?

And how can you do so while actively seeking connection rather than just "picking up your check" and leaving?

I think connection is the balm of joy. We were not meant to do without this ingredient. We were simply not built to live this life alone. Anytime I know I have made an impact in someone's life, it is like hitting the spiritual jackpot. It's like I just won the mega millions in my soul. (I hope others feel the same when they've impacted me.) There have been thousands of stories throughout #ImChangingthe Narrative that have made this abundantly clear.

I was speaking at my alma mater, Auburn University, in 2017. I shared that kings and queens (and royals) do hard things. They do things that other people are unwilling to do. They say they're sorry. They right their wrongs. They forgive people who by the world's standards would never deserve to be forgiven. They get in the ditch with people; they aren't just fair-weather friends on the mountaintop. They do the hard work within themselves. They lead, they serve, they give. They think of others first.

Yep, kings, queens, and royals do hard things. After my talk, I got the following message from an athlete:

I just wanted to let you know that I actually just had a conversation with my dad today and finally forgave him for being absent for so many years. It was mainly because I was following right in his footsteps. I was not being a king, I was just trying to avoid being like him and I ended up being just like him. Now I feel as if a burden has been lifted off of my shoulders and I can now regain focus on what God really has planned for me. So I want to truly thank you for taking time out of your schedule and allowing God to use you to speak to me. God has blessed you in so many ways and you are truly amazing!

I cried like a baby.

My first thoughts, when I got his message, went to his father, believe it or not. What he must have been thinking when he got that call out of the blue. What a gift that was laid out before him. One laden with grace, sealed with mercy, and bathed in the sweet aroma of forgiveness. Can you imagine being that father? On the other end of the phone your son tells you, "I forgive you, Daddy, for not being there for all of these years." It was a gift he surely did not deserve but one freely given by a newly crowned king, his son! This king tells me to this day that their relationship is growing and getting stronger.

If that were all there was to this story, it would still be prodigious in its impact. But there is more. Just as you cannot throw your rock out onto the pond of life without creating some sort of response, this king's story reverberated with others as I carried it on my cross-country journey presenting #ImChangingtheNarrative.

I visited another school a few months after meeting this particular king. At the very end of my talk, I told his story. Afterward, many players stayed and visited with me. They poured out their hearts. Before they left me, I hugged them and held them tight. I wanted them to know how much I care.

One of the players on this fateful night said, "You know, Miss Rachel, when you were talking about the guy forgiving his dad . . . well, I haven't talked to my mama in almost three years." I stopped him right there. I told him there is nothing, nothing that should keep him from his mama. (Let me expound here. I am a huge proponent of healthy boundaries, but I'm also a big believer in saying what you need to say, making peace, and forgiving. So even if that love is from afar, that's okay, as long as the air is clear, my dear.) I told him I would hate for anything to happen to him or to her and it be left that way, with things unsaid, and hurt and regret being the lasting emotions.

I said, "Promise me you'll call your mama."

He nodded yes with big tears threatening to fall from his eyes.

I hugged him tighter and held on to him for dear life.

Shortly after, another young man told me that his mom had a drug problem and had given up custody of he and his siblings when he was in third grade and that he had been raised by his father. I asked, "Is she still alive?"

He nodded, mutely.

"Call her," I said. "Call her, please!"

He also agreed.

Again, my heart goes to that mother. Is she still struggling with her addiction? Could a call from her child be the thing that turns her around, if she is not already clean?

I followed up with these two players just before Christmas, and I was floored and ecstatic to learn that both of them had reached out to their mothers right after the talk. Reconciliation was afoot. Families were being mended. Bonds were being reformed.

And let me remind you: love wins. It may not feel like it at the moment. The world feels dark and hateful, but in the end, love wins, and it always trumps evil. So hold tight, my love. Hold tight.

I reached out to my king with the absent father. I told him what he had done, what he had inspired. I said, "You set off a chain reaction of grace and forgiveness. Because of you, two players are going into this Christmas season with their mothers back in their lives."

He was overwhelmed with joy.

I am so grateful that the work I do has spread far and wide, not only to athletes but also to law enforcement, high schools, halfway houses, churches, and more.

If you feel a tickle in your soul, it's for a reason. God didn't call you by accident! The God of the universe has given you a purpose—your assignment—just like He gave me mine. But you have to say "YES!"

If you feel a tickle in your soul, it's for a reason. God didn't call you by accident!

When you do, you can trust that "the one [God] who calls you is faithful, and he will do it" (1 Thess. 5:24). He will bring miracles from your life.

If I'm introspective—and trust me, writing a book with all your junk on display makes you painfully introspective—that same chain reaction of grace that was set off by that brave king actually started because I said yes to God. And I'm talking set it off like Tina Turner in "Proud Mary" set it off! What if we brought that iconic Tina Turner energy to setting off chain reactions of grace and miracles in, around, and through our lives?

All it takes is two little, but potent, words: send me.

> Then I heard the voice of the Lord saying, "Whom shall I send? And who will go for us?"
> And I said, "Here am I. Send me!" (Isa. 6:8)

I said those words when I said yes to the idea of adoption, even though it seemed absolutely insane by worldly standards. And I said yes again when I saw a problem in college athletics, which led to the formation of #ImChangingtheNarrative.

HERE I AM (SHAKING LIKE A LEAF, SCARED OUT OF MY MIND), BUT SEND ME!

What chain reaction of grace will you set off by saying yes to God? By saying, "Here I am, Lord, send me! Even if the world thinks I have lost my ever-loving mind, if You say go or do it, I'm with You, Lord! You and me, pilot and copilot, the car is gassed up. We are a TEAM! I am ready, Lord! Send me!" At least that's how it usually goes in my head because I'm trying to psych myself up.

Also, in my mind, Jesus is right beside me with "Eye of the Tiger" from *Rocky* playing in the background! I told you, I'm special! "Make your weird light shine bright so other weirdos know where to find you" (author unknown).

I can't even begin to quantify who needs you to say yes or who is on your future path and depending on you to say those two colossal words, *send me*.

That's the beautiful part of saying yes and walking in your purpose. Once you do, it spreads like wildfire.

Take this email I received back in 2017. I had to sit down, catch my breath, and marvel after reading it. (I looked up to the sky and thought, *I know that was You, God! This is all You!! How could it not be?*)

In 1974 when I was a senior in high school in a typical small southeast Arkansas town (one of those where everybody knew everybody and having secrets was impossible), a friend of mine at the time got mad at his girlfriend (also a friend of mine) on Main St. one afternoon. I stopped and got out because he had put her arm behind her back and he was trying to force her into his car. I told him to stop, whereupon he released her and pushed me in the chest (no big deal). She ASKED him to leave, he slapped her to the ground . . . whereupon I proceeded to lay him out (with one punch . . . I was in shape then).

The result: I was taken to jail by the police officer who walked Main St. in those days, witnessed the whole thing. He said I was interfering in someone's relationship. My father got involved and, well, there were no charges filed, despite the officer wanting to file aggravated battery charges on me. My dad drilled into my head from an early age that you were not allowed to even raise your voice to a woman, much less your hand. And, more importantly, if you stood by and watched something bad happen to someone and did not try to stop it, you were as guilty as the person doing it. I had a positive upbringing.

Now, to the point.

Fast-forward to 2004 . . . same couple (married now, I still don't know why she married him), same town, same street. I'm back in town visiting old friends. I hear screaming and walk out where they are into it again. I walked over just as he proceeded to punch her with his fist twice. And I laid him out again (three punches this time, I was nearly 30 years old and fatter).

The result: He was taken to jail by the police who were called by someone and arrived about the time my second punch did to his head. He was charged with abuse and did a brief stretch in the local county jail, but she did divorce him and now lives happily in another town (about 100 miles away).

I say all of this to point out how things have changed. In 1974, some in our society viewed it completely "their business" for a man to do whatever he wanted to his wife-girlfriend-whatever.

In 2004, times had changed to the point that a local businessman did a stretch in the county jail for striking his wife.

Now you are probably asking yourself, "Why is he telling me all of this?"

A couple of days ago, I ran into this guy on a trip back home (I'm on the board for the bank my mother owned) and we had a completely civil, very private conversation.

It started with, "Do you know Rachel Baribeau?" He butchered the pronunciation, but I knew who he was talking about, although I was kinda curious about what was coming next.

"I saw something she did about some narrative thing and it got me to thinking. I was wrong the way I treated (his ex), but you were the only one that ever tried to make me see that, but I didn't realize how wrong I was until I saw her (you) talking about it."

Just wanted you to know your message is getting into remote places and reaching people in some interesting ways.

You may never know this side of heaven who you are affecting. I could never even begin to fathom my message reaching a former wife-beater in a small town in Arkansas, and more importantly, changing his mind and his life, but it did.

Now imagine, my dear, what God could do with your yes. Dream big! Is there something you've previously said no to because it just seemed outlandish? Too crazy, too much? Not achievable? Did people around you pooh-pooh your dream? I want you to marinate on all of that for a hot minute, even if it makes you feel icky or sad. Now write down all the things you passed up, for whatever reason. I'm not talking about passing up tickets to Disney on Ice (although I do hear it's a showstopper for kids). I'm talking about the stuff you can't shake in your heart. The stuff that keeps you up at night. The stuff that breaks your heart. Now imagine saying "YES!" with the energy of Tina Turner singing "Proud Mary."

Imagine whose life you could change—including your own! Remember, we don't operate out of coincidence because, as Kathie Lee Gifford says in *The Jesus I Know*, there is no word for coincidence in the Hebrew language.[1] You aren't having those feelings for no good reason. I could not shake the idea of adoption for a reason. I could not look away when I saw a problem in college athletics for a reason.

You, too, have a reason! And one of the greatest joys will be hearing from you when you find yours!

One last lesson, my fellow joystarter: if you have a family or a framily (friends that are chosen family), have this conversation with them too. Teach them to say yes when it seems improbable. Teach them to listen to their soul. Teach them that, despite the odds, their yes will change the narrative and, in turn, the world.

It's never too late or too early to begin again, my love.

I am so dang proud of you. (Crying happy tears as I type this.)

I can't contain my joy. My cup runneth over. My fire burns bright. I want yours to burn even brighter, my darling heart.

JOYSTART

Spend some time sitting with and praying over what you think God might be inviting you to say yes to. Now write it down! Of course, there are the yeses he invites us to every day, but I am talking about something bigger. Something that could shape the trajectory of this next season of your life—or your life as a whole. Consider the broken things in this world that fill you with emotion. How might that need be met through your gifts and passions?

Who might you invite to join you on this journey? Maybe it's a neighbor, a fellow parent, a family member. Imagine collectively solving a problem that desperately needs a solution. Together, spend some time planning how your simple yes can make a huge difference in that space. And how can your plan prioritize connection above all else? Think strategically and practically. Give yourself some practical goals that you can achieve in the next month, and start chipping away at the problem God is inviting you to help Him solve.

CHAPTER 15

Your Ancestors

Have you ever stopped to think about your ancestors? The ones you never knew? Your grandmother's grandmother's mother or your great-grandpa times five. That's a long way back to ponder. Maybe you have their nose or their chin or the same dimple or twinkle in your eye. Maybe you laugh the same as someone you have never met. Maybe you are built the same. Genes are a beautiful thing.

There's a question I would love for you to think about as you read the next few pages. What qualities do you think your bloodline passed down to you?

When I was a sportscaster, I often pondered genetic makeup and how some families like the Mannings or the Harbaughs or the Ripkins passed down incredible athletic genes. It is just in their DNA to be wildly talented at sports (and they also all work really hard at it). I think it's also in your DNA to be hardworking or kind or a survivor. It's just a hunch, but if we can pass down athletic talent, why can't we pass down other traits and qualities? It's just so fascinating.

What's equally fascinating to me is how our souls can know we are at home in a place, a land, or with certain people. Let me explain. I am proudly Hispanic but am not fluent in Spanish. This bugs me. Actually, I am ashamed of it. Because I am wholly Latina, from my head to my toes. We Latinos love big. We love our God big, we have big personalities (both the light side and the dark side), we treasure family and loved ones big, we rest big, and we do life big. That's the best way I know to describe the Latin culture. One day, maybe by the time this book is published, I will have a conversation in Spanish with an amigo/amiga. As a matter of fact, why don't you greet me in Spanish when I see you at the book signing!

I was immersed in a city called Cuernavaca, Mexico, when I was in my midtwenties. I stayed with an older couple who were related to a friend of mine. Their kindness made my time in Mexico possible. They were just precious. I would love to go back in time and squeeze them tight just one more time. They barely spoke English and I barely spoke Spanish. But it was altogether lovely. We would often stumble through our communications, but we ended up finding ways to understand one another because our hearts were open.

I have often had these kinds of conversations in my life, the ones where you don't speak the same language but are able to communicate through the language of the heart and soul. You just get each other somehow, you know? You just know. The heart knows. But I digress.

In Cuernavaca, I stayed in the bunkhouse on the back of the property. When home, if I needed to send an email, I would go across the street to use the neighbor's Wi-Fi. I remember being at the neighbor's house, sitting at her ancient computer and typing away to my friends and family back home. To my right was a sunny courtyard with moss and greenery adorning every inch of it. On the speakers overhead, Celia Cruz—the Queen of Salsa—cha-cha-cha'ed her way into my heart. I stopped typing and looked around; the neighbor had stepped out to give me some privacy.

Suddenly I felt a peaceful sense of knowing that I was home, a feeling of home that stretched far beyond these, or any, four walls. This knowing, this belonging, was greater than any one physical place could contain; it was belonging to a land, a culture, a people. There was a profoundly harmonious waltz going on in my RNA and DNA. My organs, my cells, and my heart knew I was home.

This story reminds me of this verse: "May the LORD our God be with us as he was with our ancestors; may he never leave us nor forsake us" (1 Kings 8:57).

We had people we called family growing up, but we weren't actually related to them. Even still, I called them "my aunt," "my uncle," and "my cousin," by choice, by love. One such person was my cousin Jessica. She had cystic fibrosis. I remember seeing her protocol as a young child on the way to the beach and being taken aback. Pill bottle after pill bottle, and the pills were those huge horse pills. She gulped them down like a champ. Her mom would have to beat her on the back to clear her lungs at the beginning and end of the day. Jessica was *so* brave! Despite all of this, she was living, I tell you. I mean really living!

As we got older, she made a trip out west to Jackson Hole and Utah with me. She met a boy, fell in love—as much as you can in a few weeks. There was a wildfire while we were in Jackson Hole, so she had to stay indoors a lot. Jessica would go on to get a double lung transplant to try and lengthen her life and the quality of it. After her transplant, she started to have a hankering (a southern word that means craving) for spicy foods. She had never liked spicy foods in her life. She would soon find out that her transplant donor was a Latino first responder from Miami who was killed in the line of duty. Sometimes your cells and your organs just know. They carry your you-ness with them.

And scientists actually have a name for it: cellular theory. It states that memories, as well as personality traits, are not only stored in the brain but also may be stored in organs such as the heart (and in Jessica's case, the lungs).

Scientists have studied this phenomenon and are still discovering new things. Take the following cases that defy logic. Back in the '70s, Claire Sylvia received a heart and lung transplant from a teenager who passed in a motorcycle accident. Just like Jessica, she began to experience cravings she had never had before, like for burgers and beer. After some time had passed, she contacted the family of her donor. She was shocked to learn that he enjoyed the same foods.

Another famous case was of a young girl who received another adolescent's heart. She immediately began to experience nightmares of a man trying to kill her. Her dreams were so vivid that she went to a mental health professional who finally believed her. They were able to uncover that the donor had been murdered. The dreams were so vivid they found, apprehended, and convicted the man of murder.[1]

Wow, just wow. And we humans walk around thinking we are anything less than miraculous.

I am convinced that there are mysteries we will never understand this side of heaven, but I am excited for the day that we get to sit at God's feet, and He will explain all this to us, the mystery and wonder of our human creation. I can just imagine Him saying,

See here, I created this DNA strand in the shape of a cross. Did you know that your eyes, that I created, can distinguish between seven million colors? So next time you are in awe at the color of that blade of grass, that was Me knowing you would just love it. And it tickles Me pink. I was giving you clues all along about My handiwork, My precision, My care, and My concern when it came to making you and the rest of your brothers and sisters.

While writing this book, I felt my ancestors calling to me once again. This time it was my Native American ancestors, the First peoples, my indigenous bloodline.

I'm well aware that this might sound crazy to some folks. It also might make you uncomfortable or confused as to what being "called by ancestors" means. I will describe it like this: it's a tickle, a tug, a whisper on the wind, a gut feeling, an internal pulling to a specific land, or the draw to do something specifically. And because none of us know what really happens in heaven, besides those who have had near-death experiences, you could perceive being called in a different way. But as for me, I like to think all my people are up there together with Jesus and God "calling me."

Along with wanting to lean into my Hispanic heritage by learning Spanish, I have also felt the tug of my native ancestors to trace my genealogy; go to a reservation and observe, learn, and serve; attend a powwow; and learn how to do the sacred dances. These are just a few of the things that recently cropped up as a deep longing in my soul.

Recently, I was searching YouTube for tribal music videos and came across one that stopped me dead in my tracks.[2] I listened for a moment and immediately shut it down, knowing I wanted to play it again when I could fully focus on how it made me feel, deep down. I chose to bring it back up while sitting in my office writing. It was a particularly creative day. I was surrounded by dozens of yellow sticky notes scribbled with ideas I simply mustn't forget, little tidbits of ideas and stories that would take an okay chapter and make it outstanding and remarkable!

I was putting words to paper that I knew *you* were going to love. I was even reading my book aloud with all the treble, soul, and bass my voice could afford. I decided it was a good time to turn on this newfound sacred ancestral music. And what happened was darn near miraculous. I began to weep. Instantly. The only way I know to describe it is I felt seen, all at once, by *many* generations of my ancestors. This Scripture came to mind: "Therefore, since we are surrounded by such a great cloud of witnesses, let us throw off everything that hinders and the sin that so easily entangles. And let us run with perseverance the race marked out for us" (Heb. 12:1).

I felt their collective eyes on me. I felt all their love. It shot like moonbeams across space and time. The tears continued to course down my cheeks. I dared not move.

You've heard of *agape* love, God's immeasurable, incomparable love for humankind. But have you heard of *storge* love? The ancient Greeks used this word to describe family love, the bond among mothers, fathers, sons, daughters, sisters, and brothers.

Sometimes, we as humans have to get some distance away from an experience to reflect on and discover how special it truly is. Not this gift of an encounter. I knew how powerful and important it was the moment the first tear fell.

And now I know it was a beautiful and sacred offering from our Creator so that an orphan could feel this *storge* kind of love after all the loss she'd experienced. The gift was uniquely for me.

In the book *Captivating,* John and Stasi Eldredge talk about God knowing what you love and then romancing you with these particular things for all your days.[3] That rainbow? He knows you love them. That redbird? He knew you needed the sign. Spot a whale, sis/bro? It was just for you. He knows the innermost workings of your heart. Of course He wants to see you filled with joy. That's just how amazing He is.

But I digress in the best possible way! Let's just call it a praise break because He is worthy!

Not only were there moonbeams of love being shot at me that day, but I felt my ancestors' immense pride too. Pride from generations of people who had my nose, heart, and smile. It was so thick in the air you could cut it with a knife. I felt their genuine joy that I was alive, kicking, and breathing. I felt as if they were saying that all they went through—most likely famine, war, immigration, food shortages, slavery, their land being stolen, and every other hard thing you can imagine—was worth it. It was all worth it to see me down here making them proud. Proud that I was working so hard to leave this world a better place.

If you can imagine what a multigenerational family reunion from heaven might feel like, this was it. Their struggles were not in vain. My existence made their collective struggle worth it all. It was a message shot straight to my heart.

After seventeen minutes, the YouTube video ended, and I came back to earth. I opened my eyes and wiped my face, having just experienced one of the most beautiful experiences of my life. And then a picture of my mommy popped up on my phone as one of those suggested memories that Apple regales you with. It was a live pic so she moved, and the way she was positioned made me feel like she was staring straight into my eyes.

You may believe in coincidences, but as I've said before, I do not. I will scream it from the rooftops until I leave this planet: there is no word for coincidence in the Hebrew language. What the world calls coincidences are the very gifts God romances us with. I can just imagine Him connecting all the dots before there was time. And that's so wild if you take time to ponder it.

Just one example of what I mean. Before there was space and time, the God of the universe knew two people would meet in one of my online courses and fall in love. (I know I've mentioned this before, but aren't stories of love worth repeating?)

I know that I know that I know that this *storge* love experience was uniquely for me because back in the 1980s, Georgia Grant Baribeau (my mommy) was the program coordinator for the Office of Indian Affairs in Columbus, GA. One of her main goals was to help the American Indians of Chattahoochee Valley gain employment through job training. In an article about her work, she said she wanted Native Americans or American Indians to know we're here to serve them with social issues and job training. She said in the article that the ones she had helped had gone on to be very successful. She felt a lot of pride in helping to change their narratives and their lives. She also provided counseling services.

A physical copy of this article ended up on her kitchen table during her cancer battle. I would often stop to look at the picture of her younger self and admire how much we looked alike, but it was only after she passed that I took the time to really read it. I was astonished. You could sub our names, but the message was the same.

Love people. Lift them up. Empower them.

I am my mother's child. Her DNA lives on in me. But so does her courage and her faith and her spirit and her spunk. So does her zest for life and genuine concern for others. I can't wait to get to heaven one day and meet my far-back ancestors who have all the same qualities. Oh my, what a day that will be!

Your ancestors went through too dang much for you to give up now! As I said, they likely survived food shortages, the death of their children, joblessness, lack of viable jobs or skills to do available jobs, war, discrimination, famine, slavery, settling in new lands, the Great Depression, or the colonization of their land. These are just a few of the things they could have gone through for you to be here today.

That in itself fires me up! It makes me want to live this life with everything I've got and then some because of all they had to go through for me to be here. My mother's father died in a plane crash when she was just thirteen. She was supposed to be on that plane that day but was late coming home from a sleepover. She didn't get on that plane, and because of that I am alive. I was born. I am writing this book that you are holding. It's mind-blowing to me that because of a singular circumstance I am alive. If that trip had been decided differently, there would be no me. I bet there are many of these instances in your past as well.

The point is, your very existence is sacred! You are miraculous because you—with your exact combination of genes and family history—were born. That will preach!

I want you to read this Scripture aloud, then close your eyes and feel it in your heart!

> I knew you before I formed you in your mother's womb.
> Before you were born I set you apart
> and appointed you as my prophet to the nations.
> (Jer. 1:5 NLT)

Face it: you were set apart, you were planned. You are precious. You are worthy. You are God's masterpiece.

If your joy is waning today in a dark world, take a moment to marinate on everything your people went through and survived so that you could be here. There is (relentless) joy in perseverance. There is joy in remembering and savoring where we came from.

And there is this: maybe your ancestors didn't get to break the chains of generational addictions, abuse, habits, or curses. Maybe they never got to do all they wanted to do or be all they wanted to be, but you will! YOU WILL!

There is (relentless) joy in perseverance. There is joy in remembering and savoring where we came from.

If this is you, repeat after me: "I will do and be everything that they did not get to be! I will travel and sing and dance and heal because they didn't get to (for whatever reason)."

I am often comforted by the following quote by Angeles Arrien:

> In many shamanic societies, if you came to a medicine person complaining of being disheartened, dispirited, or depressed, they would ask one of four questions: "When did you stop dancing? When did you stop singing? When did you stop being enchanted by stories? When did you stop being comforted by the sweet territory of silence?"[4]

Maybe your ancestors didn't get to dance because they were too busy surviving, or maybe they were taught that anything other than work was lazy. Maybe they experienced so much sadness that they stopped singing.

Well, sing, my dear. Sing for your ancestors who were voiceless or forgotten. Dance, my love, for those who came before you who struggled to experience joy in this life. Dance and sing and tell stories for them—and for all the people who will come after you!

There is joy in the breaking of chains but also in the love that your ancestors are sending you from the heavens! They are rejoicing that you can and you will accomplish all your heart desires!

I see you!
I love you!
I believe in you so much!

JOYSTART

I want you to think of your ancestors and revisit what you think your blood-line passed down. Make a list of these things. What gifts and positive qualities do you know came from your forefathers? Are there things you were sent to change in your family line, generational curses you were sent to break? I'm talking huge multigenerational messes passed down from one child to the next. What if you were sent to end that cycle? What if it stops with you? That power to change the narrative is within you! You are a chain breaker!

When you are done, journal about what you hope to pass on to the generation after you and what patterns you hope to see broken. Consider asking God for His help in this process and ask Him to reveal some practical steps to start breaking the negative chains in your own family line.

CHAPTER 16

No Coincidences

J ust before Christmas in 2020, my then-fiancé and my bonus
daughter Libby were walking through our locally owned pet
store in Amelia Island. They saw a kitty cat up for adoption
named Georgia (my mother's name) and took a picture to send
to me. I took this to mean Libby wanted the kitty cat. My bonus
kids have had rabbits, turtles, and even a parrot. I tell no lies. My
eldest daughter to this day wants a ferret, but I have to draw the
line somewhere, people.

I initially protested saying, "No one has time to take care of a
kitty." But as it usually does, my heart softened and I took that as
a sign. I consulted with Christopher, and we decided that the kitty
would be a surprise gift for Christmas. When we picked up Georgia
from the pet shop, I saw her brother, Camo, there too.

Two is too much, I told myself. I mean, one already felt like a
stretch with the way Christopher and I travel. But my dang enormous heart got the best of me again, and I was back at the amazing
pet store (shop local, people) to adopt her very-bonded brother.

My bonus kids were so happy on Christmas to get these cats. They still are. We all are. That is until these kitties started bringing live animals into the house. LIVE ANIMALS, PEOPLE! My little rescue dog, Buddy Jo, had a doggie door that the cats had learned to use. One day as I was getting ready in my bathroom, I saw a slight flicker of movement on the counter to my right. I shook it off, thinking it was nothing and went about getting ready. Reaching to open my makeup bag a moment later, I saw it!

Y'ALL, THERE WAS A SNAKE IN MY MAKEUP BAG! It was not poisonous but who ever-loving cares?! THERE WAS A SNAKE IN MY MAKEUP BAG!

I started hollering and screaming so loudly that my stepdad ran in, thinking I was being attacked. He rescued that likely frightened snake as I cowered in the corner.

And then there was the time that the cats were in Buddy's dog bed. After returning from the grocery store, I leaned down to pet one of them on their back, eventually touching their tail. *My, that's a weird-feeling tail,* I thought.

It then dawned on me that it was indeed not their tail. It was a beat-up black garter snake my cats were laying on for fun! What jerks. I jumped and got so much air that I nearly landed on my countertop! My husband was out of town, and not another human soul was in the house. I called—more like scream-called—my sweet neighbors/best friends and they came over and extracted the likely traumatized snake. I was over it, done! *No more surprise visitors,* I thought as I made plans to close up the doggie door for good. My nerves were as frayed as downed power lines after a monumental storm. I was jumping at my own shadow.

But those cats had one more surprise for me.

Christopher was out of town, and the kids and I were home. It was a school night, so I set myself four alarms to make sure I mastered the morning routine for each one of them. When my alarm went off, I was groggy but raced upstairs to get Libby, the baby, up for school.

I opened her door confidently and turned on her light. She was sleeping in that downward dog position that kids often do. (My yoga people will feel me here; it's a comfortable position!) I proudly announced, "Time for school." (Simultaneously, my non-verbals were shouting, "Tadaaaaa! I got you up. I'm here for duty. I did it!")

"Rachel," Libby exclaimed tiredly, "it's 3:30 a.m.!"

What the heck, I thought.

I heard the alarm again, but it wasn't coming from the phone I held in my hand. It was coming from downstairs. I turned off her light, profusely apologizing, and made my way downstairs, rather sheepishly I might add. Turns out, it was not a device making the noise, but it was indeed an "alarm." I found there in my foyer two small, circular mounds of hair just screaming and my cats inspecting nearby. All manner and method of curse words flew from my mouth. (Sorry, God!) It was a rant Chevy Chase would be proud of. My heart raced.

I am not cut out for this cat-mom thing, I thought.

I woke up another child, my at the time sixteen-year-old bonus boy, Brooks. We ascertained they were baby squirrels and set about getting them a heating pad, sugar water, and a box filled with blankets. (Brooks has the *best* heart.) That morning, bleary-eyed after little to no sleep, I set about calling local rescues until I got in touch with Jonathan Howard, owner of the Ark animal sanctuary. I made a plan to get the little guys out to him later that morning. (Turns out they were brother squirrels, most likely knocked from the nest in the night.) Those dang cats carried them right past me as I slept. How dare they?

I was amazed when I pulled up to the animal sanctuary. The Ark had so many enclosures and so many rehabbing animals. Jonathan proudly showed me around. There were raccoons, bobcats, and lots of deer. There were red fox and silver fox, squirrels, flying squirrels, turtles, tortoises, skunks, otters, beavers, ostriches, and more.

They started doing rehab in 2011 for orphaned, injured, or abandoned wildlife. He shared with me the genesis of this extraordinary place. "So we rocked and rolled along for a year or two. And the problem is with rehab wildlife, you have three choices. In 180 days in the state of Florida, you have to release the animal into the wild, which is our goal. If the animal cannot be released for some reason, it has to be euthanized or placed with a facility that will accept it. But there are really very few facilities that will accept wildlife because there's no vet history, no medical history. And zoos typically don't take them because they could bring a disease into their facility. So I talked to a friend of mine at work and in 2014 we formed the Ark Wildlife Care and Sanctuary, a nonprofit facility where the animals that couldn't be released would have a forever home. We are currently up over eighty permanent animals."

Have you ever gotten the feeling that you are in the presence of an angel walking this earth in human form? At that moment, I knew that's what this humble man was, an angel disguised as a normal everyday human being.

I visited again to bring my bonus daughter Libby to see the animals. She loves animals. He told us another miraculous story that confirmed my earlier suspicions about this man.

"We had a girl come out to the sanctuary," he said. "She had volunteered with us before, a wonderful young lady. She wanted to take her senior pictures at the facility with all the animals. She brought a photographer and her mother, and we went out to shoot pictures with the animals. God puts everything there for a reason. We had shot some of the photos with some of the animals and I had what's called an axis buck—a spotted male deer. He was a big boy. He'd already been through the mating season or the *rutt* as they call it. He wasn't aggressive. I'd had him going on three years. He was just like a big puppy.

"We went into the pen to do the shoot with him. I was in there beside him when the girl came into the pen. Something set the buck off. It might have been when he bumped a steel rod as I was holding his antlers, but I am not sure. Anyhow, he turned on me and started attacking me. While he was attacking me, this young girl grabbed a piece of pipe that was there and tried hitting him to get him off. Because of what she did, he spun his head around and nicked her with his horns in the lower abdomen. I was able to grab him and get him off of her, and nobody else got hurt. But sadly he had to be put down because he might have killed me.

"There was something miraculous that came out of the story though. The girl who had been nicked had a small puncture wound in her abdomen. When she went to the hospital, scans showed a cyst in the exact spot she had been nicked. She was only eighteen years old! It may have cost the buck's life, but you know what? Some people think there is no such thing as fate, but the older I get the more I know everything happens for a reason. I know God orchestrated these things to happen so that this girl could potentially survive. It's the butterfly effect."

The butterfly effect basically states that the world is deeply interconnected, so much so that one small occurrence can influence a much larger, more complex system.

The small occurrence that day—a normally calm buck getting spooked—led to a young lady's life being saved. And that's not all! She is on a pre-vet track and still comes back to volunteer at the sanctuary. And the butterfly miracle of that day went even further. The young woman's mother was a trauma nurse and recognized when Jonathan didn't that he was mortally wounded. She was able to stop the bleeding until he could get to a trauma center.

Jonathan went on: "It's not the first time stuff like this has happened either. I got remarried in 2009, and we went on vacation in October. It was my wife's and my first vacation together. We went to the Keys for a few days. While we were there, I wasn't feeling good after we had gone out to eat. We checked me into the hospital, just to be safe. There was only me and one other patient. The hospital staff did a CT scan and a couple other things to see what was going on. Afterward, I noticed the doctor at the nurses' station. He picks up the paperwork and kind of rubs his forehead a bit. *Somebody's gonna get some bad news,* I told myself.

"The doctor walked into my room and handed me the paper. 'We're pretty sure you have food poisoning, but I'm gonna need you to read this,' he said.

"The printout read, *'mass, right kidney, 99% probability renal cell carcinoma,'* and I'm like, 'What does this mean?'

"'You have cancer,' the doctor told me.

"Newly married and I got food poisoning that ultimately let me know I had cancer. You believe that? Oh, and did I mention it was also my birthday?"

You know how in cartoons characters are often depicted having to pick their jaws up from the floor from shock? That was me and Libby. We were in awe at his miraculous story. I am so happy to report that Jonathan is cancer-free now. Apparently, God thought he had a whole lotta living to do and more animals to save.

"The funny thing is," Jonathan said, "it never dawned on me to quit caring for these animals. I grew up as an avid hunter, an avid outdoorsman. I've hunted all over, but just something changed when I found out I had cancer. But God saved me from that cancer for a reason. And if the reason is to save these animals, so be it. The day I was attacked by the buck, I spent a couple of days in the trauma hospital. I had a broken knee, broken elbow, and multiple puncture wounds. But I didn't quit; I went right back to the sanctuary and started taking care of them again. There's no feeling like it. You get an orphaned or abandoned baby you know can't survive on its own. You're able to nurse it back to health and put it back in the wild where it belongs. It's giving something back its freedom, something that was meant to be free."

That's the good stuff of life, perspective with a side of immense gratitude. I long to live like Jonathan. I think we all should.

I love this quote from *Good Omens* by Neil Gaiman and Terry Pratchett:

It used to be thought that the events that changed the world were things like big bombs, maniac politicians, huge earthquakes, or vast population movements, but it has now been realized that this is a very old-fashioned view held by people totally out of touch with modern thought. The things that really change the world, according to Chaos theory, are the tiny things. A butterfly flaps its wings in the Amazonian jungle, and subsequently a storm ravages half of Europe.[1]

The Bible also alludes to the butterfly effect. It says in the book of Hosea,

> They sow the wind
> and reap the whirlwind. (8:7)

In short, your decisions have far greater consequences than you could ever imagine, and seemingly random events in your life can set off a chain that leads to immense change. If that girl had not decided to do a wildlife shoot for her senior portraits, she may not have found that potentially cancerous tumor until it was too late. If Jonathan did not go to that specific restaurant and get food poisoning, he may not have discovered his cancer in time.

If we hadn't decided to adopt sibling cats that tried to murder baby squirrels, we would have never met Jonathan Howard. And I would be robbed of knowing this angel and visiting the mecca he made for all these precious animals.

I could go on and on. I see this pattern everywhere in my own life. Sometimes, I imagine if Christopher hadn't chosen to come down to the meeting I was speaking at the day we met. He has since shared with me that he was absolutely bushed from his day at work and only came

In short, your decisions have far greater consequences than you could ever imagine, and seemingly random events in your life can set off a chain that leads to immense change.

because his business partner had repeatedly asked him to. I shudder just thinking about it! I like to believe we still would've met in some other time and space, but the way it played out was just so magical.

"I never would have met and fallen in love with your mom," Christopher now says playfully.

Honestly, though! I count my blessings that my mommy got to meet and love Christopher, Leah, Libby, Brooks, and Beck. So anytime my family brings up my momma, it just slays me in the spirit.

One time, Libby piped up from the back of the car, "You have GiGi's hands." (When my mom became a grandmother, she went by GiGi.) Of course, I cried at Libby's words. I cry at everything. My eyes leak, my soul leaks (joy), and, to borrow a phrase from Bob Goff in *Love Does*, I hope I "leak Jesus" too.[2]

So keep those tears coming! It is part of what it means to be human! And I would have never gotten to cry those sweet tears of joy had Libby never gotten to study GiGi's hands.

It all connects, people!

When my flight is delayed or I'm stuck in traffic, I've learned to calm myself down and thank God for what He might be up to or might be protecting me from. I'm not always successful at shifting my outlook in the moment (I'm human like everyone else), but it's the kind of perspective that keeps me grounded. Even though we will not always know God's reasoning this side of heaven, we can still thank Him for each new day and trust that He has our best interest at heart.

Christopher caught a cab back from the airport once during a tough moment in our marriage. I was waiting when the minivan cab pulled into the drive, desperately wanting reconciliation and peace. The back door slid open and I glimpsed my husband. I tried to fill the void between us by shooting intense love beams from my eyes. The driver also got out and started walking around the front of the cab. *Weird*, I thought.

The driver then said to me, "Christopher has told me about you, Rachel, and your marriage. We talked the whole way back. He loves you very much."

I started to weep right there with the sun setting on our faces.

He kept going. "May I pray for you two, right now?"

"Yes!" I proclaimed, maybe too enthusiastically.

But, real talk, can we ever be too enthusiastic about our marriages or the relationships that mean the most to us? Because I would much rather be the person that took it all too seriously, made too big of a deal, loved too hard. I'd rather believe "too much" in the redeeming love of Jesus Christ and in the enormous fragility and beauty of the human spirit. Oh yes, my darling, count me in for *too much*, because too little is a waste of the breath in our lungs and a total disservice to the life force emanating from our chests.

So we put our foreheads together, my husband and I, and this angelic cabdriver—who was an answer to my prayers—wrapped his arms around us and prayed right there in our driveway. He prayed over us as a couple; he prayed for unity, love, and peace and for our covenant bond to be evermore. I could feel the anger and hurt dissipate between us as he spoke heavenly blessings over us. And what's even more miraculous, my husband had tried three times to get an Uber or Lyft. This man and his cab were Christopher's last resort. But as it turns out, this was a God-planned encounter. Before the man left, he shared that he was a former addict, saved by grace, but still in the midst of a transformation. I stopped to ponder this as I watched him drive away.

What if this man had resisted God's calling to get out of his van? What if he had thought, *I'm not healed enough to minister to them.* Or *You're sending me, God? What can I share with these two humans about their marriage, Lord? You must have the wrong guy.*

But he didn't.

He listened. He obeyed.

And because of it, he was a messenger bringing a sign I so desperately needed in that moment. A sign that God was with Christopher and me in our time of need, *working all things together for our good* (see Rom. 8:28).

JOYSTART

Your joystart today is centered around investigating and marinating—like a good steak—in all the things that have created butterfly effects in your own life. Write them down and start to notice the fingerprints of God guiding the events of your life.

I also want you to consider how God might want to use you to start setting off chain reactions of His goodness in the lives of those you encounter. Whether you know it or not, you have experienced your own butterfly effect and can set one into motion with even the littlest act of kindness. You are a walking miracle waiting to happen. Time to start acting like it.

What good will you do with this realization?

When I am out speaking, I ask this question: "What sets your soul on fire?" I can almost see the wheels turning in people's minds as they think on their answers. So I will ask you the same thing: What are you most passionate about? We were all created differently. What moves you may not hit me the same way, and that is okay! What you saw and experienced as you grew up has shaped your heart and soul. Don't ignore those indicators.

I think that far too often these days when we try to change the world through volunteering or giving back, we aren't working out of our sweet spot. Because of this, it is far easier to get burnt out. We volunteer or we quit just to check the box and say we did it. We do only what is required, and we never return to the task or movement. I'm asking you to take a deeper look at *why* you serve and what it is that you care the most about.

If you serve in your sweet spot, you'll never get tired of giving back.

The world needs more people operating from their sweet (servant) spot. Can you imagine what we could get done in the world if we were all on fire with our purpose? It would be incredibly powerful.

I have had people tell me things like, "Miss Rachel, I saw homeless twins under a bridge when I was growing up. Ever since then, I have wanted to start a homeless shelter." That is operating from your sweet spot—using your story to spark in you a passion to meet a need.

Or "Miss Rachel, my sister has autism. I dream of getting noise-canceling headsets into all sports stadiums so all autistic people can enjoy the game."

That is taking life experience and letting it mold you for the better.

Spend some time considering what your sweet spot might be—where a need intersects with your passion, gifting, and story. Write down a few examples of what you think might set your soul on fire. Then try some of them and see if any are a fit. Take stock of what moves you. When you find it, give your life to it and set the world on fire with your good deeds!

Conclusion

We have gone on quite the journey together, dear heart, and while it feels like the end, it is anything but that. It is just the beginning of living on a different plane, a different frequency. What you have learned here is a different way of walking and talking and treating other human beings. Maybe you have already started to apply these principles in your life—I'm stoked if you have—but if you've been waiting until the end to absorb it all, the time to act is now!

WE ARE THE JOYSTARTERS!

There is a great meme going around the internet about starting a gang—the good kind—and getting matching jackets. Joystarters, you can bet your bottom dollar we are going to get matching jackets (and hats while we are at it). In fact, we are going to rally all of us joystarters together from all over this land and change the narrative. (We actually started a club: www.joystartersclub.com.) First, we will radically love ourselves in a way that is so light, so wonderful, and so magnetic that others will want that same kind of healing. Then, we are going to take that same love and spread it out into our families, our schools, our towns, and our communities.

The whole premise of this book is about finding and cultivating—and continuing to find and cultivate—joy in a world that can be oh so dark. And if we are the joystarters, it's up to us to teach ourselves, and then others, how to hold on to and chase joy relentlessly.

And here's the thing: once you picked up or downloaded this book, you automatically belonged to the club. No one is getting left out around these parts. We are an inclusive bunch. We will be meeting up at book signings, retreats, and events across the world! My hope is that maybe, in part because of this book (and our new club), you will choose to be a part of (or create) service projects and organizations that matter to you. (Serve from your sweet spot, remember?) In doing so, you will change the narrative of your communities in ways that cement your legacy and start a fire in your soul. Because there is nothing more beautiful than a soul on fire!

And what would warm my heart even further? If you teach your babies to be joystarters too, no matter how old they are. You are never too old or too young to be who you were created to be! Teach them to love themselves and love others. Even better, show them by your example. I cannot wait to hear your stories of success, life change, forgiveness, and oh the miracles you are going to start to notice and fully experience. I hope you start book clubs and send me pictures of you wearing your jackets and hats.

Thank you from the bottom of my heart for joining me on this journey! Writing this book has been the hardest, most beautifully cathartic experience of my life. I told my amazing book editor Rachel McRae that I don't think there is anything I'm prouder of in my life, save my family. I have cried all over my computer and taken less showers than I care to admit. I have had to relive hard and horrific experiences, but in the end, they hurt a little less—and I count that as joy! On the flip side, by writing this book I got to relive some stunning moments in my life; so for that I also thank you.

In the span of time it took to start the book proposal, write several chapters, and hand in the manuscript, I went from hiding and healing in the safe cocoon of my best friend's basement to being married and having a family of my own. God has done a beautiful work of restoration in that short amount of time, and the book you find here is better off for it.

If He will do this for me, He will surely do it for you.

Thank you endlessly for buying this book. It means everything to me. Your purchase is proof that you haven't given up. Stay the course, get your shovel, and do the work.

And have faith, even if it wanes at times. If you hold tightly to God, you will achieve things beyond your wildest dreams.

Here we are at your new beginning. The next chapter is yours to write.

In my family, we don't say goodbye. We say, "See ya when I see ya." It makes the parting sting a little less. So, see ya when I see ya!

But I'd love to hear from you. Shoot me an email: Book@RachelBaribeau.com. And hey, a reminder: I open my own email!

And one last time for now . . .

I love you!

I see you!

I'm holding space for you!

You are AMAZING!

I am endlessly proud of you!

You got this! Get back up if you must!

And please don't struggle alone, my darling!

With all my heart,
Rachel Joy Baribeau (Rohe)

Acknowledgments

First and foremost, I want to thank Jesus Christ. Without Him, I would not be alive to tell my story. I can now look back and see how every single step was for His glory and pointing toward this book.

To my mommy in heaven, I've felt you every step of the way, Tooty, right there on my shoulder, loving me and encouraging me. Oh, what a day that will be when we are reunited. Thank you for making me the woman I am today and being the inspiration for this book. And to my adopted father, David Baribeau, thank you for choosing me and giving me your last name and your heart. I'll see you soon, Daddycakes. Y'all give Mr. May and my soulmate of a grandmother, Opie, a giant bear hug for me.

To my husband, Christopher William Rohe, thank you for covering down in every way so I could hole away to write. You made this book possible with your selfless actions. Thank you for being the most honorable, dependable human being I know. Not to mention, you are HOT and my beloved!

Thank you to my (bonus) kids. You gave me encouragement and space to write this book. I know I had to miss out on things to make this happen, but you showed me grace! Leah, you are so very brave and strong. I can't wait to watch you take on the world. Libby, thanks for remembering GiGi and always making me laugh. I love your knowing, tender heart. Beckham, you inspire me with your relentless nature. Keep striving for the best in every single thing you do. Brooks, you are a man, my son, and what a fine one you are. Keep leading by your actions. There are lots of people watching you, and you influence them greatly for good. Each of you makes God proud. Stay close to Him in all you do.

Thank you to Aunt Karen, Mama Nish, and Mama Jackie for stepping in after my mommy passed and being shades of my mother. I needed you desperately. Thank you for loving me as a daughter.

To my brothers, Matt and Todd, my aunts and uncles, and my cousins (and extended family), thank you for covering me, loving me, and cheering me on all these years. A special thank you to my Uncle Michael for naming me Rachel Joy.

To Gary, thank you for teaching me the game of football and for being my dad. To John, I am beyond grateful for the relationship we have built. Thank you for giving me life. And to Daddy Bryan, you have loved me since I was born. Thank you for being a father figure to me.

Thank you to Jeannie and Tate for giving me the apartment to cocoon and recover and for the home-cooked meals and love.

To my (forever) bridesmaids and friends that are family, you make my life's tapestry so very rich. Thank you for choosing me to do life with you (and your babies). You know who you are! I love you!

Thank you to Pastor Derwin Gray for being faithful and diligent in telling me I was *supposed* to write this book and then promptly connecting me to Alexander Field at the Bindery. Thank you to Estee Zandee for believing I had this book, and many more, inside me and guiding me in the process of developing and pitching while simultaneously helping me mend a broken heart. Thank you to Drew Tilton for lovingly helping me edit my baby (this book) and making the manuscript shine. You are my brother in Christ and an ally in creativity. Thank you to Trinity McFadden for the guidance and support I needed at just the right time. Thank you endlessly to Rachel McRae, my editor at Revell. You have been my cheerleader, shoulder to cry on, crisis manager, sister-in-Christ, and soft place to land. I adore you endlessly. We did it!

And thank you to the entire team at Revell. God brought me to the perfect spot in y'all!

Thank you to Jason, Patricia, Emma, Matt, Lindsay, Dr. Josh, Brandy, Linda, Tre, Allison, Kim, Abby, Nichola, Natasha, Lee, Darrell, Jennifer, Reina, Soloman, Verkedric, and Jessica, my team at #ImChangingtheNarrative, for the support while I wrote this book. Each one of you is an absolute rockstar, and I love you to the moon and back.

And a huge thank you to my friends P.J. Fleck, David Tyree, Laura Rutledge, and my mentor, Coach Bill Snyder, for lending your name to this book.

To each person who let me tell their story in this book, THANK YOU! I wanted to call you by name, and you let me. One million thank-yous would not be enough!

And to my (joyful) tribe, THANK YOU! This is for you—for each person who has loved me, encouraged me, prayed for me, and opened their heart to me and my message! I wrote this for you! I love you!

Notes

Introduction

1. Joseph Stromberg, "The Microscopic Structures of Dried Human Tears," *Smithsonian*, November 19, 2013, https://www.smithsonianmag.com/science-nature/the-microscopic-structures-of-dried-human-tears-180947766/.

Chapter 1 The Birth of a Movement

1. Rachel Baribeau, "College Football is Breaking My Heart," GridIronNow.com, June 2016. This article and website is no longer available.

Chapter 2 People First

1. Og Mandino, "The Motivational Speakers Hall of Fame," Get Motivation, accessed October 19, 2020, https://www.getmotivation.com/ogmandino.htm.
2. "About Og Mandino," Og Mandino Leadership Institute, accessed October 31, 2022, https://ogmandino.com/about-og-mandino/.
3. Jennifer Delgado, "Affective Presence: Did You Know We All Have a Unique 'Emotional Signature'?," Psychology Spot, accessed October 19, 2022, https://psychology-spot.com/affective-presence/.
4. Delgado, "Affective Presence."

Chapter 3 On a Hill in Africa

1. Jonathan P. Baird, "Remember Martha Gellhorn? Here's Why You Should," *Concord Monitor*, November 27, 2019, https://www.concordmonitor.com/Remembering-Martha-Gellhorn-30393393.

Chapter 5 The Gift of Pain

1. "The Most Brave and Terrifying Thing I've Ever Shared #ChangingtheNarrative," YouTube video, 11:33, posted by Rachel Joy Baribeau, July 11, 2019, https://youtu.be/Kb_TVlsHPzY.

Notes

Chapter 6 The Garden Tomb

1. Story adapted from memory and Zieva Konvisser, "Viner, Yochanon," Zekelman Holocaust Center, June 4, 2015, https://www.holocaustcenter.org/visit/library-archive/oral-history-department/viner-yochanon/?fbclid=IwAR0ljrjylHxU664UbpXSaJkO9RE-zj1kR8W2xBiwNV5WArj0OB-SQCXBWl8.

Chapter 9 Feed Your Soul

1. Andrea Watkins, "Benefits of Deep Breathing," Urban Balance, November 3, 2014, https://www.urbanbalance.com/benefits-deep-breathing/.

Chapter 10 The Pity Kiddie Pool

1. CrisMarie Campbell, "How the 20-Second Hug Makes All the Difference in Your Happiness," Thrive!, September 4, 2018, https://www.thriveinc.com/post/2018/09/04/how-the-20-second-hug-makes-all-the-difference-in-your-happiness.

2. Kelli Anderson, "Kay Yow 1942–2009: After an Inspiring Fight, a Beloved Hall of Fame Coach Succumbs to Cancer," Vault, February 2, 2009, https://vault.si.com/vault/2009/02/02/kay-yow-19422009.

3. Donald Miller, *A Million Miles in a Thousand Years: How I Learned to Live a Better Story* (Nashville: Thomas Nelson, 2011), 14.

4. Vince Gaia, "Cities: How Crowded Life Is Changing Us," BBC, May 16, 2013, https://www.bbc.com/future/article/20130516-how-city-life-is-changing-us.

Chapter 12 In His Time

1. Gary Chapman, *The Five Love Languages: How to Express Heartfelt Commitment to Your Mate* (Chicago: Northfield Publishers, 1992).

Chapter 13 Miracles in Disguise

1. "Frida Khalo and Her Paintings," Frida Khalo, accessed October 26, 2022, https://www.fridakahlo.org.

2. Matthew (@CrowsFault), "People speak of hope," Twitter post, March, 10, 2021, 2:21 p.m., https://twitter.com/crowsfault/status/1502001835779014666?lang=en.

Chapter 14 It Starts with a YES!

1. Kathie Lee Gifford, *The Jesus I Know: Honest Conversations and Diverse Opinions about Who He Is* (Nashville: Thomas Nelson, 2021).

Chapter 15 Your Ancestors

1. Gianna Absi, "Is the Brain the Only Place That Stores Our Memories?," *The Nerve Blog*, November 11, 2014, https://sites.bu.edu/ombs/2014/11/11/is-the-brain-the-only-place-that-stores-our-memories/.

2. "Heal Your Soul: Ancestral Chants from the Native Americans," YouTube video, 17:46, posted by Ancestral Way Music, May 3, 2020, https://www.youtube.com/watch?v=WaMP7a17OsY.

3. Stasi Eldredge, *Captivating: Unveiling the Mystery of a Woman's Soul* (Nashville: Thomas Nelson, 2021).

4. Angeles Arrien, foreword to *Maps to Ecstasy: The Healing Power of Movement* by Gabrielle Roth (Novato, CA: New World Library, 1998), xv–xvi.

Chapter 16 No Coincidences

1. Terry Pratchett and Neil Gaiman, *Good Omens: The Nice and Accurate Prophecies of Agnes Nutter, Witch* (New York: Workman, 1990), 205.

2. Bob Goff, *Love Does: Discover a Secretly Incredible Life in an Ordinary World* (Nashville: Thomas Nelson, 2012), 142.

Journaling Space

Journaling Space

In 2016, groundbreaking national sportscaster **Rachel Joy Baribeau** penned a piece for GridironNow titled "College Football is Breaking My Heart." The game she loved was becoming unrecognizable. Negative news stories dominated the game, and no campus seemed immune. Most broadcasters would have left it at that.

Not Rachel.

Rachel developed #ImChangingtheNarrative with student-athletes in mind and a belief that one crooked course made straight is everything. One misstep not taken means one less victim in the world and one less life thrown away because of a split-second bad decision.

At Rachel's first visit, sometimes people are skeptical when the petite Latina woman is introduced as the speaker, but in just sixty minutes she wins them over. She now speaks to athletic groups, law enforcement, churches, and corporations about taking back the headlines for good—showing them that they have the power to change the narrative and to find their purpose in life outside of their sport and everyday lives. To live lives of . . .

Purpose, Passion, and Platform.

Just like her inspiration, Alabama and NFL star Kevin Turner, did before he succumbed to ALS and CTE.

When she's finished, people wait in line to speak to her. They tweet, private message, and text her. They trust her and report back on their efforts to become the kings and queens she consistently challenges them to be. While the message originated as "purpose, passion, and platform," more than four-plus years and forty campuses later—and as a victim of domestic violence herself—it now heavily encompasses mental health, being a king or queen every day of your life, and interpersonal relationships.

When she is not traveling to speak or teach, Rachel adores taking naps, dancing in her kitchen, visiting museums, learning about history, and spreading joy on a daily basis. Of all the titles she goes by, she loves "wife" and "bonus mom" the most. She lives in Florida with her family and fur-children.

MEET RACHEL JOY BARIBEAU

Rachel is an inspirational speaker and coach as well as
the founder of #ImChangingtheNarrative. She is committed
to living with passion and helping others find their God-given
joy. Learn more about her story and current projects
by visiting **RachelBaribeau.com**!

PURPOSE, PASSION, AND PLATFORM

#ImChangingtheNarrative is a movement that brings positivity and purpose to students, professionals, and parents across the country by focusing on mental health, self-care, leadership, social justice, and interpersonal relationships.

Interested in joining the movement or inviting Rachel to speak to your school, company, or agency?
Get connected at **ImChangingtheNarrative.org**.